Staying Grounded

—— in ——

Shifting Sand

Also by Dr. Linda J. Ferguson

Path for Greatness: Spirituality at Work

Other publications include articles and chapters in:

Interbeing: Journal on Personal and Professional Mastery

The Workplace and Spirituality: New Perspectives on Research and Practice

See also her weekly blog on spirituality and work:

www.managementhelp.org/blogs/spirituality/

Staying Grounded

—————— in ——————

Shifting Sand

*Awakening Soul
Consciousness for the
New Millennium*

Linda J. Ferguson, Ph.D.

BALBOA
PRESS

A DIVISION OF HAY HOUSE

Balboa Press books may be ordered through booksellers or by contacting:

Balboa Press
A Division of Hay House
1663 Liberty Drive
Bloomington, IN 47403
www.balboapress.com
1-(877) 407-4847

Because of the dynamic nature of the Internet, any web addresses or links contained in this book may have changed since publication and may no longer be valid. The views expressed in this work are solely those of the author and do not necessarily reflect the views of the publisher, and the publisher hereby disclaims any responsibility for them.

ISBN: 978-1-4525-4121-1 (sc)
ISBN: 978-1-4525-4122-8 (e)

The author of this book does not dispense medical advice or prescribe the use of any technique as a form of treatment for physical, emotional, or medical problems without the advice of a physician, either directly or indirectly. The intent of the author is only to offer information of a general nature to help you in your quest for emotional and spiritual well-being. In the event you use any of the information in this book for yourself, which is your constitutional right, the author and the publisher assume no responsibility for your actions.

Any people depicted in stock imagery provided by Thinkstock are models, and such images are being used for illustrative purposes only.
Certain stock imagery © Thinkstock.

Printed in the United States of America

Balboa Press rev. date: 11/21/2011

Looking behind I am filled with gratitude.

Looking forward I am filled with vision.

Looking upwards I am filled with strength.

Looking within I discover peace.

Apache Prayer

Table of Contents

Preface

What started as a follow-up to my first book, *Path for Greatness*, extended into an adventure of my own spiritual journey. It became clear that as I moved through my spiritual tests, I was provided the opportunity to learn, apply, and practice the spiritual ideas I was writing about. What wondrous ways God presents us gifts!

I have had the marvelous opportunity to meet, hear, and learn from many amazing souls who are sharing their gifts with the world. Numerous writers have influenced my thinking over the years, so I have included a Reference section at the end of this book as acknowledgement and gratitude for their work.

I know I can't thank them all here, but I would like to highlight several friends who have helped me in my journey over the last decade and supported my work on this book. The Sequoia Sisters—Nancy, Freeda, Sheila, Diane, Lizbeth—held the sacred container for our sharing and stretching. Maggie, Terry, Debbie, Elizabeth, Kim, Greg, Lindsay, Joe and Neil each in their own way supported my personal growth and journey so that I can do this work today. Suzann, Rev. Diane, Azurae, Rev. Alec and Rev. Beth offered many hours of rich conversation and study that supported the development of these ideas. My extended family, including my wonderful nieces and nephews, continue to enrich my life.

Through my work with coaching clients and workshop participants I developed a process called Transformational Empowerment$_{\text{T.M.}}$ I am indebted to their feedback, ideas, and sharing so that I could clarify my thinking. My work continues to evolve.

When we do the deep transformative work in our own life, we feel empowered and energized to step forward fully as the magnificent expression of our Divine Essence. If you are reading this book now, you too hear the calling to follow your soul journey and to share your unique gifts with the world. I offer this book and the Transformational Empowerment process as a tool to help you radiate your Light. I hope you'll find ideas here that are meaningful and useful in your journey of self-exploration, conscious co-creation, and soulful living. I feel honored and privileged to share my work with you.

Linda J. Ferguson
Sept. 2011

Introduction

Happiness cannot be traveled to, owned, earned, worn or consumed.
Happiness is the spiritual experience of living every
minute with love, grace, and gratitude.

Denise Waitley

Readers of my book, *Path for Greatness: Spirituality at Work* told me they wanted more. I had said all that I had to say. Well it's amazing what a few years of life experiences can teach us about how to move along our spiritual path. Besides my own personal transformative work, I've been privileged to hear many wonderful stories in the course of sharing my work with groups all across the country. Readers and workshop participants emailed or called to tell me how my book, *Path for Greatness,* helped them integrate their spiritual life and their work life.

Still I was hesitant to write yet another treatise on how one lives an awakened life. What could I possibly say that hasn't already been said before? However, if people understood how to walk the Path of Love based on what has already been written or taught, we wouldn't have the turbulence and violence that we see today. The world would be a far more peaceful, consciously loving place if people knew and practiced the ideas contained in the writings and teachings of the ancient or contemporary sages. All the great faith traditions teach how to live in Love.

The following story highlights why I finally accepted the idea that I should write this book.

A synagogue had called a brilliant young rabbi to be their new teacher. Everyone was thrilled with getting this young man because his reputation as a thinker and teacher was well known. In his first service he gave a brilliant message and the members were very pleased they had hired such a fine teacher. The next week the rabbi presented the same message. Some of the members of the synagogue scratched their heads and thought maybe the rabbi had forgotten he had said the same thing the week before. After the third week when the rabbi presented the same message, some of the members of the synagogue went to the elders questioning whether the young rabbi indeed was all that he was built up to be. When the fourth week the rabbi presented the exact same message the elders knew they needed to approach the rabbi. The elders pulled aside the rabbi after services and said that they really liked his presentation style and that they were waiting for him to share more of his insights with the congregation. The rabbi simply smiled and said, "When you've truly gotten the first lesson, I'll move on to the second one."

The primary lesson is that we need to remember that we are spiritual beings here on this earth journey to consciously evolve to greater levels of Love. Your soul chose your unique particular life for your greater growth and beauty. How you walk your path is up to you. Your conscious evolution involves learning your key soul lessons, learning to offer and receive Love, and staying connected to your Divine Essence.

The better able we are to awaken to our soul journey as we navigate through our physical world and daily living, the more we can share our Divine Essence. We are each here to love and to share Love unconditionally.

Great masters and teachers throughout time have offered ideas for enlightenment. So what does this book offer that is new? Perhaps nothing. But I hope that I might include some stories or insights in just enough different ways for you to continue on your journey. This book, like so many others written over the centuries, attempts to illuminate key spiritual lessons and help you consciously re-commit to your soul journey.

As I explained in the introduction of my first book, the way I use language here is important. References to personal pronouns will be alternated such that "he" may be used in one sentence and "she" in the next. The intent behind this is to be as inclusive as possible and to avoid focusing on one particular gender when making a point.

Because there are so many interpretations and characterizations of a divine power, I want to be explicit in how I am referring to such a power. Specific words that are capitalized throughout the book refer to the "Abiding, Abundant Love that goes by many names yet is beyond naming." This is done in recognition that one word for this Presence is too limiting. When I use the term "God Consciousness", I am referring to this presence and power of Love that we each can access when we are fully open to receiving it.

This book is meant for those of you who are seeking a path of enlightenment, self-actualization, and spiritual integration in your life. It is meant for those of you who have felt pain deeply enough to change something in your life or wish to experience greater joy in your life. It is for you who have experienced the call for personal transformation and want to learn how to make it stick. It is also a reminder text for those already on the path of being a Light unto the world and perhaps in need of a bit more inspiration and rejuvenation in your work. Jack Kornfield wrote another excellent book on this subject *After the Ecstasy, the Laundry*. It was an important book for me to read and it helped me strengthen my resolve to make my personal transformations stick.

In the pages that follow I will share more stories of my own journey and others' transformative work. I will expand upon some of the ideas in my first book and offer more ways for finding or regaining your center even in the midst of chaos or upheaval. Ultimately this book is about integrating spirituality into daily life. It occurred to me while speaking to a group about my first book that it could have been titled "Life as Spiritual Service". Your life needn't be mundane or meaningless; it can be so joyous and rewarding you can hardly contain that joy. It requires persistence and commitment to follow the path of Love. Learning how to live a life of spiritual service will help you follow your path of Love.

Many people unfortunately can't fathom being a light for others because they are in such a place of pain or woundedness. For too many people just surviving another day is a major challenge. We must help others find their inner light and share our own light along the way. Perhaps you are reading this book now so that you can be such a guide or torch bearer.

I was introduced to the singer songwriter Chuck Brodsky about a decade ago and I love these lyrics "We are each other's angels, and we meet when it is time. Go answer the calling, go and fill somebody's cup. If you see an angel falling, won't you stop and help them up."

Thank you for picking up this book and trying out the ideas. Thank you for continuing on your journey towards inner peace and transformation. Thank you for being a Light for the world.

> *Come, Come Whoever you are. Wanderers, Worshipers, Lover of Leaving. This is no caravan of despair. It doesn't matter if you've broken your vows a thousand times. Come Yet Again Come.*
>
> Jelaluddin Rumi

Part I—Foundation

"I wish I could show you,
when you are
lonely or in darkness,
the astonishing
Light of your Being."
~Hafiz.

CHAPTER 1

❦

The Awakened Path

Life as a free and fortunate human being is precious because it
gives us the opportunity to cultivate the awakened mind.

His Holiness, the Dalai Lama

I traveled to Asia several times and in one trip had the opportunity to visit Nepal. One of the excursions was to the Royal Chitwan National Park, a former hunting ground for the king. It is open to the public for walks, jeep rides or elephant rides to see the wildlife in its preserved state. The national government allows a limited number of people to enter the park with a guide, which entails crossing a crocodile-filled river in a wooden canoe.

One early morning walk, we came across a couple of rhinos bathing in a small pool. Our guide told us to lay low since the rhino will charge if it senses danger. Our guide also explained that rhinos have very poor eyesight, and so if it sees something move it will charge regardless of the animal. Rhinos have even attacked jeeps. Our guide seemed to take delight in calling to the rhinos to get their attention and then back off when the rhinos looked around or moved. The rhino is a good metaphor for those who are living their lives without a fully awakened mind. Many people sense danger and attack, even if they don't fully understand what they are attacking. And because they can't see clearly, they feel in a state of anxiety or danger most of the time. You may know such people. They could be co-workers, neighbors, community leaders, friends or family members.

The fight or flight instinct is very strong in us. Fight or flight, along with feeding and mating, are the four basic human instincts. When stressed we react out of instinct or deeply learned patterns. We react without thinking through what may be happening, or as the rhino, without seeing what's really going on. Luckily we humans can stop from instinctive, knee jerk reactions. We can reflect on the situation and see it from various viewpoints. Staying open and aware you needn't simply react. You can choose how you respond. You can attack or flee or you can negotiate, cajole, charm, or surrender. As we move from childhood to adulthood we learn to see situations beyond what is immediately happening and to consider various options for dealing with life events.

A spiritually awakened mind not only determines what is going on in the material physical plane, but also sees beyond what is happening in the immediate moment. You learn to look for and eventually understand the spiritual lesson or spiritual drama being played out. Everyone can cultivate this spiritual way of seeing to become more centered and grounded in the midst of turbulence or stress of daily life.

It is too easy to lose balance by the stresses of daily living, to let our small self call the shots, allow other people's agenda and ego, or our own fears, run the show. The question is—what game do you want to play? Do you want to play the game of life that feeds that small self or do you want to play the game that expands yourself? The bigger game involves seeing where your growing edge is, moving beyond your routine daily living to re-connect with your soul journey. You need to be willing to open to the Cosmic wake-up calls and nudges of your soul to learn the lesson required and find more solid ground. This is a game that lets you tap into power much larger than your small self and achieve possibilities beyond your wildest dreams.

The awakened mind entails seeing your physical, material world in addition to another world where you view life events metaphorically or metaphysically. Life events to the awakened mind are opportunities to grow, learn and experience joy. With an awakened mind you'll learn to love more deeply, forgive more, offer compassion at every opportunity, be joyful, and find grace in any given moment.

If you aren't ready to live with an awakened mind, then stop reading now. Just put the book down and walk away. If you aren't sure, keep reading.

For, to paraphrase Alice in Wonderland (and it was such a good line in the movie "The Matrix"), once you go down this rabbit hole, you'll never look at the world the same way again.

Great mystical traditions through the ages have described the magnificence and wonder of beholding the Divine Beloved, even if for a fleeting moment. Great reformers, spiritual teachers, and avatars through the ages have tapped into this powerful force, moving past earthly illusions. If you are reading this book you probably have consciously and intentionally sought this path. Congratulations to you. Welcome home!

Cultivating your awakened mind and using it as a daily spiritual practice takes commitment. You'll likely experience obstacles and hardships as part of your life journey. These challenges can scare you back into your sleeping state if you are not paying attention. Your smaller self, scared ego, complacency all can easily carry sway in your journey. It helps to have a good support network or supportive loved ones to stay on the awakened path. If you want to expand your world and your life beyond measure, the awakened path provides many rewards.

In this book I will review ways to progress on this awakened path. It all starts with answering the stirrings of your soul, saying, "Yes!" to the magical mystery tour of life.

> *It all starts with answering the stirrings of your soul, saying, "Yes!" to the magical mystery tour of life.*

The awakened path allows you to live your life more fully integrated and to accept all the life events you experience. You can surrender your worry and anxiety, moving through your fear and grief to new levels of peace and vitality. For centuries mystics and sages have described the experience of awakening, transcendence, and enlightenment. Many images for the awakened path include piercing the veil of illusion of this physical world. Plato's allegory of the cave teaches that there is more to life than watching shadows on the wall—greater understanding comes from stepping behind the shadow. Buddha became enlightened by sitting under the Bodhi Tree, emptying himself of all his previously held desires and beliefs.

The search for deeper understanding and the meaning of life has been part of human experience since before the written word. Staying grounded in shifting sand requires that we look beyond what is happening, and see the spiritual process that is unfolding. In essence, staying grounded requires playing the game of life by following spiritual rules as well as the well-trodden earthly material path, with its rules for living and dying.

Too many in our society are caught up in scarcity consciousness or superiority mentality rather than an abundance and interdependence consciousness. Unfortunately the mass consciousness hasn't fully learned the lesson of how to live by the basic tenets of Love. We all need to learn, practice, or refine our "awakened mind" to make such a world possible. We're seeing the ramifications of our not learning in dramatic ways globally, from deforestation and global warming to sweatshops and exploitation during times of enormous wealth and advances in science and medicine. The global economic meltdown of 2008-09 is the result of greed and corruption on a global scale. It demonstrates that we are all interconnected and that our solutions will be found not through legislation but with a change of heart and soul.

I began writing this book in 2003 during the early stages of the US war against Iraq. It was a time of great anxiety, confusion and uncertainty in our country and around the world. The economic crisis of 2008 only amplified this global uncertainty. The title of this book fits these times perfectly. How are we to stay centered and balanced in the midst of confusion, chaos and uncertainty? Even if our own life is going fairly smoothly, we will encounter others who are feeling anxious or angry, and we will have to deal with their pain or troubled emotional state. We are called at this time to find ways to achieve inner peace that can be brought out into our world. Indeed one of the most important spiritual rules is that we create our world from the inside out—how we respond to others (fear vs. love), how we hold on to ego or call in Divine Guidance—all determine what world we create.

A friend of mine wrote me an email during the first months of the Iraq war about learning the core lesson of peace. He wrote, "This war has taught me much about peace. I'm seeing that my anger over the war is no better than the anger of those waging it. When it comes right down to it, everyone is doing the best he or she can do. I have come to rest in that awareness and now I am the peace around which I had been dancing." What a beautiful insight!

This new perspective of my friend is precisely what we need to learn, not just for our own inner peace, but to truly transform the world. Bullies and terrorists exist, not just on a global or national scale but also in people's work lives and in their own homes. September 11th 2001 was a dramatic global wake up call. The economic meltdown of 2008 similarly hit people where they could feel the pain. These events are cosmic two-by-four planks smacking us across the face to wake up and live differently. Will we continue to slumber or use this wake-up call to make lasting transformation for the planet? In his book, *"Creating a Meaningful Life,"* Bo Lozoff urges us to get off the fast lane and into the vast lane. The vast lane awaits those of us ready to move into it. The game of expanded consciousness and awakened mind is there if we accept the call to play the game.

I've been fortunate that my book tours have allowed me to meet incredible people who are taking their awakened path seriously. They are committed not just to doing the same old same old. They are courageous enough to examine their own past programming and unhealthy patterns in order to release themselves and move forward. My journey the last few years has been likewise. As a result of my divorce shortly before my first book was published, I went into the depths of previous pain that I didn't know was there. I doubt I would have 'voluntarily' created the situations to address my deeper wounds. But life gives us those opportunities to do our most important work; indeed that is the essence of our soul journey. And this is the basic condition of the spiritual game of life—you will always get what you need for greater spiritual growth. It may not come in the way you want or expect or in the time you desire, but you get experiences to heal your wounds and face your fears. You always have opportunities to move to greater love, compassion and forgiveness. The work we're here to do is to clean up our own house so that we can be more present and loving to those as they try to clean up their inner house.

Following the awakened path you develop a sense of lightness and openness that you've never experienced before. It also will require that you face your fears and self-limiting beliefs and clear them out. This can be scary work but ultimately leaves you much freer and easeful since you won't spend as much energy reacting from a place of woundedness or fear. Learning to be present to the pain and joy in life requires that you learn how to take it all in as it arises without guarantees, attachments, or judgments. If you are a Type A, High Need Achiever person (as I was), this can be a challenging task.

To follow the awakened path you must have courage and faith. A spiritually grounded friend of mine offered me this definition of faith—"Faith is the substance of hope and the demonstration of things not yet seen." Through faith you know you are never dealt more than you can handle. Faith helps you accept that your lessons come to you as you need them and that your experiences are opportunities for growth for your highest good. The opportunities for such learning come when you are ready to experience them, even if you aren't so sure you can handle what is happening. As much as you might like to skip certain lessons, either because they are too painful or you want to jump ahead a level, the steps happen in the right progression for our highest learning. It is also important to remember that you each have your own particular soul progression. You cannot know for another person what lesson they need to learn or the sequence of their lessons.

When you see events happening from a spiritual perspective, you can dig deeper to find the greater lesson of what is going on. Indeed you can give up judgments of "right" or "fair" about things happening in your life. The rake of pain may cut across you, but the sweet touch of Spirit tends to your wounds. Events occur in perfect timing, even if you can't see the bigger picture at the time. Once you give up attachments and your judgments of right and wrong, you can accept more freely what flows through your life. From this place of detachment you can give and receive Love more freely. Releasing attachments to how you think things "should be," frees up an enormous amount of energy that otherwise would be used to fight off an enemy, prove you are right or worthy, or cover your wounds.

Another handy tool for the path of awakening is courage. It is difficult to step out into the unknown, to change beliefs or patterns of behavior. Many people don't want to give up the comfort or convenience of life as they know it. There is safety in the familiar, even if it is unhealthy or not leading to the life you want. People stay stuck in their view of themselves as victims to life's events. They don't know how to or don't have the courage to make those changes. It really helps to have a guide or mentor who can help.

Acceptance is another helpful tool for this game. The quicker you learn to stop fighting what is occurring in your life and open up to the gifts that are presented, the quicker you move towards wholeness. It's tempting during these trials to feel like a victim or even abandoned by God. Yet it is through your trials that you gain new perspective, develop compassion, and allow Divine Presence to shape you. Or as the maxim goes, "God prunes us now and then to make us fruitful." With each pruning you go to the next level in the spiritual game.

Many simply haven't experienced self-acceptance, personal joy, or the trust of others and thus move through the world in fear. Those who continually live in fear bring their struggles, woundedness, and confusion to the world. It is all too easy to ricochet off each other's unbalanced energy. You feel the effects of it in your daily life. The key to stopping these wobbly ways of living is to find the tools and anchors to keep grounded. If you are tired of this wobbly way, there is another path.

Those who choose the awakened path often bump up against the status quo. If you have always known you were "a little bit different" perhaps it is because the awakened path called you at an early age. For others who have lived in the mainstream and yet shifted somewhere along the way, it is really scary. All of a sudden you don't connect with others around you, you begin to question long standing accepted "truths" or challenge others in their ways of thinking. You find yourself wanting something more, something different, something more rich and meaningful and substantive. Following the awakened path doesn't necessarily preclude physical comfort, security, or material wealth. It does require that you look at all those things you stay attached to. You will come to understand that following your soul's progression means being more conscious and intentional with your daily decisions.

One cautionary note: *This journey is not for the weak hearted.* It entails going into depths of uncertainty and darkness that many people simply don't want to experience. Yet sometimes you find yourself in that place of wandering or suffering and don't know how to stop it. Often the awakened journey begins with a trauma or major jolt to your system. If approached with an awakened mind, such a life event provides an opportunity for you to re-examine your life.

Following the awakened path often entails releasing your attachments to those things and beliefs that have anchored you in the past. Perhaps this release will be voluntary or perhaps you will experience an involuntary release that you are trying to make sense of. If you are questioning basic beliefs about your life or have to rebuild your life after a major loss, find comfort in knowing it is all part of awakening. It's all part of being more aware of and tending to your soul's journey.

A very dear friend lost her home in New Orleans from Hurricane Katrina. Four months later she moved her family back to a rental apartment to try to rebuild their life. A week after she moved back she found out she had breast cancer. She could have given up or gone into deep depression or despair. Instead she faced what she had to do with her usual spark and determination. By facing her ordeal with confidence and humor, she created more positive encouragement for her family and friends so they would not lose hope. And five years later, she is cancer free.

> I developed a new prayer-'May my lessons come more gently'.

When you follow the awakened path you will find that you aren't rocked as hard when tough times occur. As an awakened being you will respond to challenges with greater clarity and strength. You will be able to embrace the times of doubt and darkness rather than fight them. As you learn to be more aware you won't need such dramatic or intense wake up calls to pay attention. A few years ago, as I began to really live the awakened path, I developed a new prayer-

'May my lessons come more gently.' I've found on the whole that they have, or at least that I've been able to learn the lesson more quickly so I can return to a more balanced and grounded life.

Part of the game is realizing that your life won't be all bliss once you learn an important lesson. You get continual opportunities to practice this lesson. The awakened path often puts us more in touch with deeper emotions that have been buried for so long. You may feel even more intense pain or sadness. You may be even more sensitive to the suffering of others. But as you do your own healing and growing, you are more able to live with the pain and move through it more quickly. Like the bobo doll that rocks back to center when hit squarely, you come back to balance and wholeness more fluidly when you learn the way of the awakened path.

There's a fabulous story of a group of Englishmen who had moved to India in the early part of the 20th century. They were homesick after many years in India and so decided to build a golf course there. They talked with other Englishmen to lay out the course and were able to get some clubs and balls shipped to them.

Of course these Brits hadn't taken into account the different terrain and animals in India so converting the sport of golf was quite challenging. Frequently monkeys would wreck havoc on their game by scrambling down nearby trees and running off with their golf balls. After weeks of trying to scare away the monkeys, throw their golf clubs at the monkeys, trap them, and bribe them with other food, the monkeys still made the game impossible.

The monkeys in turned loved this new game of golf. They most loved to pick up the balls and throw them down the course and chase after them. This only made matters worse for the golfers.

Finally after many months of trials and tribulations with the monkeys, the Englishmen decided to just accept that the game of golf would be different in India than back home. So to accommodate the monkeys, they realized they needed new rules for playing the game. Over time they created new rules and learned to love the game. Golf now had lots of new twists and possibilities. The rule that helped them find comfort and enjoy the game was this—"*Play the ball where the monkey drops it.*"

You'll find much greater peace, comfort and perhaps even joy, if you too learn to play the game of life as life happens. Accepting life on life's terms is an essential ingredient to staying grounded in shifting sand. By following your spiritual journey with an awakened mind, you return to your inner anchors and regain balance much quicker when you get rattled.

To Start the Game—Sign the Learning Agreement

There is a learning agreement that is part of this earthly journey. You may have just an inkling of what that is at this moment, or you may have known it for some time, even your whole life. Yet there are certain lessons you have to learn in this lifetime. For some of you it may be harder to learn about forgiveness, for others it may be harder to learn generosity. The toughest lesson for us is offering unconditional love and releasing judgments of others or ourselves. The opportunities to learn these lessons occur every day, or could be just around the corner. In some cases they will appear in periods of significant life transitions. The best way to determine your life lessons is to look at recurring events that seem to trigger similar emotional responses. Look at those life situations and the outcomes that have touched you deeply, whether it is pain or joy. Those tend to give clues to your soul journey.

I spent more than a decade trying to discern my path and had only glimpses of what lay ahead. Yet similar patterns of my soul's journey and purpose kept emerging. As Spirit works, when the time was right for me to become more aware of my soul journey the next important life experience occurred. If you are experiencing some major emotional or physical shifts in your life, such as a job, health, or relationship transition, you are being given the opportunity to gain insights into your learning contract. Stay open to what is being revealed in what you are experiencing now in your life.

Too many of us have learned to discount our intuition. Our society puts so much emphasis on external validation of truth that you dismiss your own inner knowing. Worse yet, we rarely teach children nor did we learn as children how to trust our inner wisdom. While schools spend time in science classes teaching methods of empirical examination to learn objectively verifiable aspects of the physical world, we don't formally teach methods to discern inner truths. At certain times, we meet people who teach us how to discern our inner knowing from fleeting emotions or impulses.

At the end of this chapter you'll find a set of questions to help you uncover what your spiritual learning agreement may entail. I recommend you take some time to go within, be quiet, and open your heart as you complete the learning agreement. You might want to do a meditation or visualization first to get your mind open to reviewing your life. Another option is to put on some music that helps you clear your mind and just sit with each question without writing anything at first. Work through them as often as you need to discover what your soul journey entails.

Staying grounded in shifting sand involves paying attention to your daily life experiences and seeing them with new awareness. The awakened path is a continuous process of intentional daily living. I used to think that after I made one transition to a new level of awareness I'd be set. Now I recognize the spiraling dimension of life, moving to greater levels of awareness and growth yet circling back to similar issues. With each pass of the spiral I gain new insights and humility, and find new ways of being connected to others to share and experience Love. Such is this spiritual game of life.

I invite you to pay particular attention to the types of people you seem to draw into your life. They are here as your guides and teachers. They may have helped you through joyful and loving experiences or through painful and difficult ones. The people brought into your life in significant ways are there for your growth and learning, and on a soul level, you've agreed to do important healing or transformative work together. Enjoy life as it unfolds and keep your heart open. It is all part of your awakening process.

End of Chapter Exercises

Discovering your Learning Agreement:

To Start the Game, discover your learning agreement. Open up to it, step fully into it. The journey awaits you.

1. What thoughts continue to trouble you (block you from experiencing inner peace)?

   List out as many as you can (e.g., anxiety about money, fears about safety, worry about what others think, feelings of inadequacy etc.)

2. What life events have triggered the most change in your life? List them in as much detail as you can so that you can see them fully. How did you feel? Who were the people involved? What roles did they play? How were you involved in shaping or creating the life events? What decisions did you make as a result of the event?

3. When someone really pushes your hot buttons what thoughts and emotions arise?

   When you experience great joy, what images of yourself come to mind?

4. Look over your answers to questions 1-3. Are there patterns of events that trigger similar emotions in you?

5. After reviewing all of the above, what lessons do you think you are here to learn?

Learning Agreement—

I recognize and accept that I have a soul journey to take on this earth walk. By staying open to my soul journey, I welcome those who come to me as teachers, healers, guides, and support.

I recognize and accept those situations that trigger pain, loss, disappointment, and sadness for they serve to open me to greater love and compassion.

I see that I still need to learn: (List your discoveries from the reflective exercises above)

I choose to move through these experiences with an awakened mind and caring heart.

With gratitude for the beauty, wonder and love that is provided in my daily life, I welcome learning new ways to live in greater love and joy. I graciously give what I am here to offer for my own and others' happiness, healing, and benefit. I choose to walk with greater peace, sharing my joy and love freely with others.

In accepting this learning agreement, I allow my soul journey to accelerate by experiencing ever more moments of grace. I accept this learning agreement on a conscious level to fulfill my soul contracts as they are presented.

_____

(Name)

_____

(Date)

CHAPTER 2

༺༻

Spirit and Matter as One

If I could persuade myself that I should find God in a Himalayan cave, I would proceed there immediately. But I know I cannot find God apart from humanity.

Mohandas K. Gandhi

One of the greatest struggles and most important mission for our life is learning to live simultaneously in the metaphysical realm and the 3D physical realm. The best way to stay grounded in shifting sand is to integrate these two realms in daily life. As you develop your spiritual practice and stay connected to your Divine Wisdom, you get the insights needed for your soul progression.

The spiritual realm refers to that non-physical, metaphysical space that is beyond external sensory validation. It includes the sixth sense of intuition, soul wisdom, and guidance from Master teachers, angels, totem animals, and the like. The earth realm is the physical, material, three-dimensional, five-sensory world. You can know and experience both worlds if you remain open to them. If you close off your awareness of the non-physical world, you miss out on information, guidance and support that can be helpful for daily life. I take as a starting premise that we are spiritual beings in human form. Our body temple houses our soul.

Rather than bouncing from one realm to the other, I believe our central task on this life journey is to live in the physical world while staying connected to the spiritual realm. Though great yogis and master teachers through the ages have been able to remain connected to God Consciousness every moment, most of the rest of us cannot. Our daily dramas and personal agendas trip us up. Not only is it unlikely that you can stay connected to God Consciousness all day long, very few people believe that's the point of their life. Most people do the daily living and that's all. They don't know there is a soul journey unfolding. However, being so focused on ego demands and wanting, you forget you are a spiritual being. If you don't pay attention to your spiritual life you will feel depleted and frequently stuck. Connecting the two realms, using spiritual guidance for your human experiences, you are best able to stay grounded in the shifting sands of your physical world <u>and </u>progress on your soul journey.

Some people prefer to play in the metaphysical realm and don't ever master the earth realm. They run into continual struggles with housing, jobs, relationships, health or finances. Others only focus on the earth realm and never master the spiritual lessons, moving through life trying to dominate or control others, or taking advantage of others for their own gain. You are here to master both realms and integrate them in your daily life. As you master this integration of both realms, you can move more easefully and gracefully through your life conditions, making the most of each experience.

Seeing all of life as an expression of the Divine is an ancient viewpoint. It is one that each generation seems to have to keep relearning. As you more consciously and intentionally integrate the two realms you can help others awaken to their soul journey. Many on this awakened path feel the quickening happening in their own lives and around the planet.

The Old Paradigm of Dualism

The dualistic notions of Spirit versus matter, Divinity versus humanness are deeply embedded in Western culture, yet are not found in mystical writings or indigenous cultures. Mystical traditions and indigenous cultures have integrated these two realms and hold on to them despite the colonization of Western ideologies and life styles.

A dominant Western world perspective today is that there is a spiritual destination (many call this heaven in one word or another) existing some place outside us. Actually you can "return home" (experience the oneness with God, Nirvana, Enlightenment) at anytime when you remember you are not separate from the spiritual realm. You can create heaven on earth by remembering that you are a Divine Being in physical form. Thus our greatest challenge is not to *find* God in daily living, as though God was hidden somehow, but to recognize that our daily living is the expression and experience of the Holy Oneness. This involves remembering that we are the embodiment of Universal Love.

> *You can create heaven on earth by remembering that you are a Divine Being in physical form.*

When you are only focused on your earth walk and fail to connect with your spiritual Source, it is easy to mistakenly believe Yaweh has forsaken you in times of struggle or pain. Unfortunately many people still believe they have done something wrong and Yaweh is punishing them for their actions. This notion of Yaweh as punisher for wrongdoing is a good tool for those who want to control other people's behavior.

Let's look at a classic parenting situation—a child spills milk at the table. When this happens do you automatically go into judgment mode and tell her how careless or stupid she is? Do you feel you need to punish her for it? Another approach is to simply point out what she did to spill the milk and ask her how she might be able to prevent that in the future. Get her to see how she can handle a glass of liquids. She will learn the consequences of not paying attention around full glasses and will correct her own behavior. No judgments or punishments are necessary. The logical consequences of the situation ("if I'm not paying attention I can spill milk") take care of the problem. Your life conditions help you learn effective ways to handle your challenges—when you pay attention. Judgment and condemnation are not necessary.

When you experience pain from acting out of ego, you feel the natural consequence of not feeling connected to Source. It is not because there is some force acting upon you from the outside that is punishing you.

We humans do a fine job creating our own suffering; we don't need a divine being to do that for us! You don't need to judge others or yourself as acting certain ways. You need only notice whether what you are doing is effective or ineffective in staying connected to your Divine Essence. If you stop paying attention to your Higher Power and focus instead on your own small self, and ego based ways of being, you lose touch with your Spiritual guidance. You put too much attention on getting what you want to serve your ego and forget that you have abundant guidance and support to experience your Divine Essence. God does not punish us for doing anything "wrong".

All your pain, turmoil, or illnesses are reminders to seek out more ways to love, offer compassion or surrender your self-serving ego. Stop blaming others or yourself for being or doing wrong. Instead, recognize your soul is calling you to forgive others and yourself when they or you fall short. This is pretty radical thinking, but as you learn to see life as a soul journey, it is true.

Inner struggle comes when you are not clearly expressing unconditional love. Inner peace comes from complete acceptance of what is, acting from a place of love and grace. The more people act out of ego and not from their Divine Essence, the more their turmoil expands. Again there is no judgment necessary of whether you are good or bad, worthy or unworthy. There is just recognition of whether you have worked in alignment with your Divine Essence or not.

When the physical world controls your life, you'll have to let go of things that are precious to you to find inner peace. Even when you live in alignment with your Divine Essence, there are times when you will feel pain or loss. Remember, such experiences are for your soul's progression. The bottom line is to not judge or be mad at others, or feel forsaken by God when you feel pain or experience loss. You may not get exactly what you want the way you want it or in the time frame you want it, but you are offered grace every day. In fact sometimes the best thing that could happen to you is <u>not</u> getting what you want.

The Divine Plan for Peace on Earth is made more concrete as you are able to express Love. As the famous passage from St Francis of Assisi goes, "Make me an instrument of Your peace." Heaven is not a place that is a physical destination, it is a state of being, a conscious knowing you are a Divine Expression. Your soul journey and your daily life are separated only to the degree to which you believe in that separation. Though we often speak of living in two worlds (spirit and matter), in fact it is all Divine Essence in various forms.

Influential early Christian leaders such as Augustine taught that people should deny the body and focus instead on the life of the spirit. This dualistic view, Spirit as separate from body, influenced western Christianity and Western culture for centuries. It perpetuated the message that people should not pay attention to their physical well being because somehow that takes away from tending to one's spiritual well being. It also resulted in a greater emphasis on the after-life than the earthly world.

Christian religious and political leaders oppressed their followers for centuries by emphasizing that heavenly rewards were to be found later so don't worry about pain in this lifetime. This doctrine still perpetuates personal slavery for many who have learned to view their body as lowly. The lack of integration of body and Spirit results in lack of internal wholeness.

Buddhism also addresses earthly experiences and suffering. The Buddha's first two noble truths are that life is suffering and suffering occurs when we are attached to the material world and our own desires. The key to breaking this suffering is to transcend the earthly attachments. Many Buddhist monks sought refuge in their spiritual community, the Sangha, as a way to practice disengaging from earthly attachments.

Nicheren Daishonin was a twelfth century mystic and Japanese Buddhist priest who taught ways to move through 'human revolution" that did not require people to be unattached to earthly concerns, but honor each experience as it occurs. By chanting a phrase that he believed to be a distillation of most important Buddhist teaching from the Lotus Sutra, anyone could overcome not only current life conditions but also alter one's karma (cause and effect) from previous life experiences. The phrase "Nam-myoho-renge-kyo," according to Nichiren, would help to shift life conditions and karma by tapping into a mystic law that pervades all existence. There has been a revival of Nicheren's teaching since World War II as Japanese war brides brought this tradition to the West and Japan rebuilt itself as a democratic society.

Contemporary Buddhist teachers have brought their wisdom to help us Westerners with everyday modern living. Thich Nhat Hanh and Pema Chodron are prolific writers and wonderful teachers of Engaged Buddhism. Engaged Buddhism involves living fully present to life not separated from it. Their teaching on mindfulness, paying attention to what is without judgments, has helped thousands cope with life's turmoil. Engaged Buddhism allows monks and lay people alike to live fully in the world. They believe that people can break the cycle of suffering right in the moment rather than waiting for lifetimes for it to be achieved.

Integrating Spiritual Realm and Physical Realm into One Reality

Those who have not awakened to their soul journey live as 3rd Dimensional beings. You may remember such a time in your life. Think of times when you've simply reacted to what was happening without understanding the 'Matrix' involved. 3rd Dimensional Beings don't believe or understand their life experiences beyond the physical events that happen. They do not work with Spirit guides, angels or ancestors, nor intentionally connect with Source/God/Higher Power in the midst of the situation.

Here is a common division of the physical and spiritual realms. Integrating these two realms means learning to live in both realms simultaneously, treating them as an integral way of life. As you progress on your soul journey to a 4th Dimensional being, you see these realms as One existence, not separate realms.

Physical realm - Human experience	Spiritual realm - Soul experience
Material	Non-physical or meaphysical
Five Senses	Extra sensory (eg., Clairvoyance, Divination)
Ego/personality	Soul lessons
Habits and behaviors	Divine Essence
Emotions	Divine Love
Want/Needs	Soul Journey agreements
Resistance or Negotiation	Acceptance of 'All that is'

You can learn about your soul journey and greater truths both through your physical senses and through extra-sensory means. Most of our education is for the physical realm, yet much can be learned about accessing greater wisdom and guidance by developing intuition and extra sensory skills. Far more is happening around us than meets the eye.

Since you are reading this chapter, you already have some awareness of yourself as a 4th Dimensional Being, integrating your physical world and the non-physical realm as a unified reality. You've undoubtedly had some experience of a presence beyond what you can explain on the physical material plane. Below are some stories that may resonate with your life experiences.

I have a friend who went rock climbing as a teenager and had a metaphysical experience. He was fairly experienced free-climbing up to heights of about 60 feet without a harness or rope support. One day he climbed about 40 feet up and grabbed onto a portion of rock. When it broke he fell off the rock and down several feet in the air. He almost started to panic as he knew he was free-falling. Suddenly he felt a support catch him and gently push him against the rock wall where he could grab onto a hold and establish some footing. There was no one on the rock wall with him. He knew he had been assisted by an angelic presence of some sort that stopped his fall and brought him back to safety.

I had a similar experience of a presence in the midst of danger. I was driving on the interstate out of Chicago with traffic moving quickly. As the cars in front of me slowed down to about 45 mph, I hit my brakes. For some reason I looked in my rear view mirror and saw a car closing in fast beyond me. I instantly thought that I was going to get hit unless the car swerved to my left. The driver did swerve but not fast enough. He clipped the back corner of my car, flipped my car on its side and sent me shooting into the next lane. I played Toyota pin ball hitting a semi-truck in the right lane, flipped onto my roof upon impact and slide back across 3 lanes of traffic. As I was sliding on my roof I had a fleeting thought that I'd better flip back onto my wheels or else I would crash into the cement barrier separating our traffic from the other on-coming 4 lanes of traffic.

In that instant, I felt a hand or presence flip my car back on my wheels. I stopped inches before hitting the cement barrier. My car was totaled, yet I walked away without a scratch. I distinctly remember the feeling of my car being pushed back upright on its wheels to avoid hitting the cement median.

Over the years since this accident, I've learned to integrate my daily life with my soul journey. I've asked for and received assistance and guidance in less dramatic situations. You may work with Ascended Masters, the angelic realm or other guides. Such support and assistance is just a thought away. Daily life challenges come and go more quickly as you learn to reach out for assistance from the non-physical realm. Guidance is more readily available as you intentionally integrate the two realms and live in them as one seamless reality.

As you increase your awareness of the physical and spiritual realms, you'll see them as an integrated wholeness. Consciously living connected to both realms, you are able to respond with greater clarity, confidence and understanding of the life situations you face. Sorting through life challenges and problems by examining them only from a physical 3rd dimensional view misses half the story.

> *As you continue to be aware of your soul journey, you'll more intentionally draw to you what is in your right highest good and fulfill soul contracts more swiftly.*

As you continue to be aware of your soul journey, you'll more intentionally draw to you what is in your right highest good and fulfill soul contracts more swiftly. Once you see the link between your soul journey and your human experiences, you start to open yourself consciously and intentionally for those beings that will help you on your journey. You stay alert to times when you are being used to help another learn something for their soul's journey. The learning agreement for a soul's progression entails a whole range of experiences and emotions. You will learn to see that your life experiences are gifts offered and guided with Divine Love.

When you connect with others deeply you are experiencing them at the human personality level as well as at the soul level. In fact those people who affect you the most, either through joy or sorrow, have soul level work to do with you. You don't necessarily have to like the person to make the soul connection. As you awaken to your soul journey, you will draw to you those who can help you in your journey. Though this connection doesn't always occur at a conscious level, with an awakened mind and the tools from this book, you can learn to recognize more quickly your soul experiences.

Seeing perfection in the imperfections of your life is really tough. In order to shift perspective you have to keep reframing how you see things. Ask yourself, "What is here for me to see differently?" Divine guidance is there to support moving through your lessons.

My friend Rev. Diane likes to use the expression "I can't wait to see how Spirit will work this one out!" I have used this expression often and it has been amazing to see the results. One time in the midst of confusion and despair, I was telling myself a story about how awful someone was acting. I caught myself getting wrapped up in my story and was able to shift gears. In the next instant I remembered a Sufi chant, 'Only love is flowing here'. I started to repeat the chant several times. In less than 5 minutes I not only felt better, but the person I was interacting with moved into a much more loving tone and we reconciled easily.

> "I can't wait to see how Spirit will work this one out!"

Traveling through your soul journey does not mean that you allow abuse or oppression to continue when you see it. You are being called in that moment to create a more loving world in whatever way you feel you can. "Surrender to God" is not an excuse for not using your talents to break cycles of fear. Indeed when you stay grounded in fear and do not work to change conditions that create fear, you are not acting according to your Divine Light. Fear blocks us from finding Divine Love and expressing our Divine Essence in the moment. Diminishing fear in your own life and in the lives of others is a tremendous step toward creating peace on earth.

With an awakened mind you will shift perspectives more readily. When you can see the soul experience in your human experiences, you will have discovered the path for integrating the two realms.

Evolving Scientific Paradigm

The Enlightenment Era, starting in the mid 1600's with the writings of Newton and Descartes, brought forth the birth of scientific methodology and empirical rigor to answer questions about the material world. The Age of Reason, as it also was called, and the resulting scientific inquiry diminished the emphasis on finding truth through intuition, prayer, meditation, or "extra sensory" experiences. This scientific fervor was a backlash against church oppression by church leaders and allied political rulers that forced certain truths and unquestioning devotion.

As a result, over the past few centuries the pendulum has swung in the other direction, with scientific analysis and empiricist approach given more credence for showing Truth and Knowledge than intuition and other forms of gaining understanding about the world. The Scientific Empirical paradigm has compartmentalized all life into measurable units discounting forces in the world that can't be measured by the five senses. It's clear what modern society values by the amount of time and money spent on scientific education and research over education in philosophy, consciousness, and world religions in high schools and universities.

Learning about greater truths has become divided terrain. Science and technology deal with matter and the physical world while religion and philosophy deal with the metaphysical, transcendent world of the soul.

Even a discipline such as psychology, which rests in the nexus point of science and philosophy in understanding the mind and human experiences, gives more credence to science and matter than to consciousness as studied by Eastern religions and philosophy. Almost every university psychology department has an empirical approach to psychology. While the word "psyche" is the Greek word for soul, it is the rare Intro psychology class that focuses on how our human experiences are part of our soul journey.

Scientific training is founded on the notion that something must be observed, measured, and manipulated to be "proven" to exist. Thus, study of the soul and of spirituality was left to theologians to debate but not seen as the domain of science. Statistical significance is the current criteria for what gets published and accepted as scientific truth. Efforts to understand non-empirical phenomenon, such as after-life experiences and soul travel, aren't seen as credible or are dismissed from being possible. Spiritual discernment and intuition are pushed aside by science as a tool for understanding the physical world.

Rationalism, an approach that came out of the Enlightenment era, shifted the paradigm of contemporary living away from believing in unseen forces acting on the world to only believing in those things that could be measured. The Enlightenment era led to the Industrial revolution and the zeal of science and technology as the way to find solutions to daily living. Certainly many diseases have been cured through science, and technology has advanced our ability to communicate and "be more productive". Most of us wouldn't want to go back to living a 19th century life.

Now science has propelled us so far forward that we have come back around to asking fundamental questions: What is life and where did it all start? Embryo and DNA research led to cloning and we are faced with fundamental questions: What is a 'natural' life form? Is there a soul? At what point does the soul exist? These questions will probably not be answered by science as we know it today.

Over the last century physics has shifted its framework away from the purely Newtonian worldview in large part by Einstein and quantum physicists. Research at sub-atomic levels of matter has ushered in the Quantum age. Though Einstein couldn't measure certain aspects of the universe, because they were either too big or too small, he proposed the theoretical methods for understanding what could happen at such distances and sizes. Due to technological advances in measuring things at extremely large or small dimensions, quantum physics today has radically challenged our notion of how things work in the world. It has expanded the scientific framework from the Newtonian "machine" model of the world. This machine model framed scientific research—all the pieces of the natural world could be understood by taking them apart and seeing how each piece works individually, much like pieces of a clock. The new scientific paradigm views the world as being at the same time more chaotic and still organized according. Now systems theories and intelligent design are paradigms discussed in science. The early 20th century physicist and mathematician Sir James Jeans proposed the continuous-creation theory in astronomy. He noted, "The Universe begins to look more like a great thought than like a great machine".

Energy as the New Paradigm

In recent years a few cutting edge psychologists, biologists, and other scientists have published works to explain how our human experience is governed by more than what we can examine and measure. Bruce Lipton's book, *The Biology of Belief* outlines biological research regarding how our bodies are influenced by our beliefs. He writes, "It is our environment and beliefs and not our gene driven hormones and neurotransmitters that control our bodies and minds". Suzann Panek Robins' book, *Exploring Energy: Cultivating Healthy Relationships through Insight and Intuition* addresses the biofield as energy centers and another tool to understand yourself and your social relationships.

Numerous contemporary writers of medicine and physics are explaining the world as energy. The works of Fred Alan Wolf, Caroline Myss, Andrew Weil, and Barbara Brennan, to name just a few, have brought greater attention to how energy impacts our lives and how you can change your life by changing your energy. Meg Wheatley refers to the "New

Science" which incorporates ideas from Chaos Theory, String Theory, Quantum Entanglement and other advances in scientific understanding. The underlying theme in all these new theories is that there is a force that provides structure to 'coincidental' events. The key element of this force is energy.

This energy is also part of our spiritual development. As we develop ourselves spiritually we operate at higher energy frequencies, and thus we can make shifts not only in our own lives but also in the physical world around us.

The scientific empirical method looks for external things to cause certain effects. In classic physics, Newton's Law of Motion states that an object in motion will stay moving in the same direction unless a force is applied to change the motion of that object. Lynne McTaggert's fascinating book, *The Field*, summarizes some ground-breaking research in quantum physics. Physicists have proven that they can split an atom sending the subatomic particles to different locations, change the spin of one subatomic particle, and the rotation of another subatomic particle of that same atom will change, even in another location! Some other force or mechanism must be operating. These types of research findings have resulted in a whole new way of viewing the material world.

The field of Quantum physics brings us legions forward in expanding the realm of Spirit (as a form of energy) into the material world. Quantum era scientists have debated the influence of an unmeasurable force, coined the "God Factor", to explain phenomena at the subatomic level. Some cutting-edge scientists now propose that there is an invisible "Field" that connects all living things.

One of the more interesting and dramatic reports of energy at work is by the chemist Masaru Emoto. He researched water around the globe affected by pollution, mounting population growth, and negative human thoughts. He reports changes in the water from fragile and fragmented crystal structures to whole and clear crystals where he and others have sent energy with focused thoughts of love.

In our daily lives we don't pay enough attention to the integration of our life energy. We seem to be over-committed for time, feeling tugs to meet needs and demands from family, friends, work, community and self. Yet when we have free time we all too quickly fill up the empty moments with another commitment or task. The latest technology gadgets only exacerbate this. Many people are not comfortable sitting alone quietly or being with others without having something to do. Thus, we don't pay enough attention to how we are using or renewing our energy.

It is easy to see the ramifications of this disconnection of body and spirit and not learning how to use our life energy. Western medicine treats illnesses by dealing with physical symptoms rather than seeking to explore energy patterns in and around our body. Drugs to suppress symptoms simply block the energy flow and may prolong the illness from moving through the body. Fever and vomiting are ways for the body to release the cause of the illness.

The remedy for many of our contemporary maladies, from illness to war, will be found in learning new ways of using energy. Homeopathic treatments for numerous illnesses are based on energy. Tinctures of elements are used in very concentrated forms that have the same energy frequencies as the illness themselves. This energy vibration of the substance in the tincture cancels out the vibration of the illness and thus the body returns to homeostasis.

Acupuncture has been used and developed over centuries based on the understanding of energy. Acupuncture works with invisible channels of energy (qi or Chi), known as meridians. The 12 main meridians form a network of energy channels throughout the body. Each meridian is associated with an organ or bodily function. In the acupuncture model dis-ease is caused by our energy (qi) not flowing easily to an organ or area of the body. Illness is treated by opening the blocked flow of energy in a meridian with a needle or tuning fork stimulation on a particular point where the qi runs closest to the skin.

Tremendous healing occurs when you remove the blocks of energy flow and allow the body to do its own natural healing work. Reiki and Healing

Touch, two forms of energy work, similarly work with helping the Chi flow more easily through and away from the body. These modalities can be used to help the body release stressors and foreign elements that cause illness.

Not only do we each have personal energy fields running within our bodies, we also have levels of energy in numerous fields surrounding our body. Contemporary understanding of these energy fields by writers and healers such as Barbara Brennan are consistent with ancient Shamanic teachings and practice of healing by working with people's energy fields.

Energy is the unifying force connecting physics and religion, reconnecting our notions of spirit and earth. There is a new field of Quantum Philosophy that seeks to reconcile the seemingly divergent worlds of matter and spirit, with energy as the new underlying universal element. Science has progressed to accept that what appears to be solid matter is mostly pure energy. Just as light is both a particle and a wave, we can shift beyond an "either-or" thinking to a "both-and" thinking when it comes to spirit and matter. Our life journey is both physical and meta-physical. We are both material energy and God Source Energy.

When you interact with someone you not only do it on a physical level but also on an energetic level. Understanding how to work with these energy levels will be key to our evolution and perhaps our very survival in the twenty first century.

Living the Divine Expression

Great mystics through the ages have described the integration of the Divine in daily experience. The distinctions of the body and the physical world separate from the Divine are most clearly rejected in the writings of the great mystic and poet Rumi. His poems speak of the great ecstasy he found in celebrating and dancing with the sweetness of The Beloved found in every day encounters.

Rumi's poetry, like other great mystical writings, speaks of the fusion of God and daily life. Mystics describe the beauty and wonder of 'All

Are One' as an expression of God to be received and celebrated through the senses. Rather than deny your body so that you can focus more on thoughts of the after-life, the mystical path embraces the body as the vehicle to experience God's splendor to its fullest.

Rumi describes staying connected to Divine presence in ordinary daily living.

> * *Without a net, I catch a falcon and release it to the sky, hunting God. This wine I drink today was never held in a clay jar. I love this world, even as I hear the great wind of leaving it rising, for there is a grainy taste I prefer to every idea of heaven: human friendship.[1]*
>
> * *You ask, "Why do you cry with such sweetness all around?" I weep as I make the honey, wearing the shirt of a bee, and I refuse to share this suffering. I play the sky's harp.[2]*
>
> * *Let the beauty we love be what we do. There are hundreds of ways to kneel and kiss the ground.[3]*

Getting past the dualistic thinking of Spirit disconnected from daily material affairs allows us to experience the Divine more fully every day. You live in a human body to experience your soul journey as it unfolds on the earthly plane. The seemingly distinct worlds of Allah and matter co-exist. Your mission, if you choose to accept it, is to open up and consciously progress your soul journey through your daily life.

While the Light of Allah is always there, our ego tests and challenges us. Similarly it is through the challenges of ego that you are given the opportunity to move away from separateness. Therefore, your daily tests provide the opportunity to reveal the Light inside you.

---

1   from *The Glance*, pg 7
2   from *The Glance*, pg 62
3   from *Illuminated Rumi*, pg 31

Awakening to your soul journey allows you to experience Divine Essence in everyday living and thus to stay grounded during the turmoil in our life. You open up more to your Divine Essence as you learn to release the blocks and barriers of your human experience. Your soul's journey is one of remembering you are a Divine Expression and stepping fully into that awareness.

End of Chapter Exercises

1. In the New Testament, Yaweh invoked "I AM" as the reminder that God is Love. When you say 'I am . . . .' what words follow in your typical day? (eg., sick, tired, disappointed, happy)

    a. Now think of yourself as an expression of Divine Creation and describe who you are by saying I AM . . . . (fill in the blank)

2. Recall a recent situation where you got defensive, hostile or felt scared. Write out the situation including as much detail as you can about what happened, how you felt, and how you and others responded in it. Review this situation and note how you react from a human perspective and with an awakened mind.

Reread what you wrote, and on a separate piece of paper do the following:

    A. Write down what judgments, perceptions or assumptions come up for you regarding this situation.

    Read each judgment and say "isn't this interesting that I have this judgment"

B. Note what physical or emotional feelings come up for you when you think of this situation. Go into your feelings and identify where in your body you hold those feelings. What lessons are your feelings showing you?

C. Which feelings and/or judgments would you like to release in order to stay more connected to your divine essence?

D. How were others in the situation helping you move forward in your soul's evolution? Bless them as they are supporting you in your soul journey.

CHAPTER 3

Integrating Spiritual Love with Daily Living

The soul is made in God's image, and when we become established in soul awareness, our personality begins to reflect God's goodness and beauty.

Paramahansa Yogananda

Learned "Rules" for Love

Everyone ultimately wants to be loved. It is a basic human need. How we feel loved varies from person to person. Usually, we experience love and love others based on how we were loved and treated growing up. We all have learned "rules for receiving love." Most of these rules were imprinted from our parents or other authority figures such as teachers, ministers or grandparents. Your awakened soul is calling you now to examine patterns of behavior that no longer serve you. While you may have needed to act in a certain way as a child to receive love or to find your place in your family, you don't need to repeat those same patterns as an adult.

You generally aren't even aware you are following these scripts or rules until someone challenges you on them or doesn't act according to how you think they *should* act. These rules or scripts for behavior play themselves out most obviously in loving romantic relationships. Even in the work place where issues of power and authority come to bear, you play out some of these same rules.

We usually get mad at people close to us when they do not live up to some of our expectations. Pay attention to what expectations you have of others and where those expectations come from. Have an honest conversation with your partner or boss about your expectations of one another so that you can learn what you each really want. In most pairs or groups, you've each learned different rules for relating to people. It's quite likely that you each have your own ideas of what a partner/friend/colleague *should* do and that might not be consistent with what the other person believes.

As you progress on your spiritual path, you're more aware that the way you treat others is connected to patterns you learned as a child. You realize what you are doing to receive love most vividly when your patterns or games don't work. Usually you get frustrated and try harder with the same stymied results. Become aware of these patterns when someone gently or not so gently points them out to you.

What rules have you learned about winning someone's love or approval? See if any of the following "rules" resonate with you.

If I love you enough, you will love me back
If I please you enough, you will love me back
I need to control you so you will love me back
I need to intimidate you so you will love me
I need to charm you so you will love me

If I dominate you enough, you will love me back
If I give in to you enough, you will love me back

Now look deeper. What do you feel you need to do so that you can love and approve of <u>yourself</u>.

If I work harder, I will be able to love myself
If I give more of myself to others, I will be worthy of love
If I do everything right, I will be good enough
If I satisfy other's needs, I will feel good about myself
If I am smart or competent enough, I will be able to love myself

Where did you learn these rules? Who taught them to you? Do you still want to live by these rules?

Here's a secret. *You don't need to do <u>anything</u> to receive love or feel worthy of love.* Breathe in deeply as you re-read this last sentence. How do you feel when you read that sentence?

> *You don't need to do <u>anything</u> to receive love or feel worthy of love.*

I want so badly to just end here. If your body tensed up or you felt a restriction or discomfort in your body as you read this sentence, you are blocking the truth of it in some way. It is our human self that has learned certain rules in the past for love and developed the patterns for receiving love. It is our human self that has received love conditionally. Our spiritual Self knows that love is unconditional and unlimited because spiritual Love is unlimited and unconditional. As a spiritual being, you are an infinite channel of Love. Love breathes through you.

When you try to find love only through the ways you've learned certain rules, you'll get caught up in the games and patterns of childhood. Your unique lessons of love are usually distorted. Spiritual Love is never distorted. It is infinite and it is unconditional. The more you can plug into and feel the presence of spiritual Love, the easier it will be to shift out of your past patterns. You can stop holding on so tightly to your learned human ways that love comes. Focus more on the spiritual Love that is limitless; by doing so you may find love not so challenging and elusive.

Spiritual Love makes no demands and sets no conditions. It flows easily and continuously; you just need to stay open to that flow. Rather than being frightened by love, perhaps of losing someone you love or not being able to get love, embrace the flow of Love; step more fully in to it. When your fear gets the best of you, if you feel your body tighten or tense up somewhere, that is the cue for you to stop, breathe and welcome in some form of Love. So here's the good news—spiritual love is an open hose that flows continuously; you just need to stop standing on the hose and let it flow.

Believe deep in the core of your being that you are ready to receive love in healthy ways. Knowing that you are worthy and that it is Okay to experience love is essential to connecting with your Source of Love. It takes an enormous amount of practice to stay connected to your Source. The best way is to begin with little steps.

> *Take a deep breath now and draw up your inner God-Sourced Love.*
> *Take a deep breath in and breathe now slowly making the sound of Hu (hooooooo) Repeat three times.*
> *Feel the breath of the Holy Oneness moving through you.*
> *Feel Love pulse through you . . . . out your hands, head, chest and feet.*
> *Imagine that this Love is radiating out from the center of your being as a violet light filling the room.*
> *Extend this Love beam to someone you care about. See them receiving this lavender light.*
> *Now send this Love to someone who is in need. See them receiving the light beam of Radiant Love.*

When you encounter a small disturbing fear, perhaps that you'll disappoint someone or arrive late for an important meeting, breathe into it and try to calm your mind and body. Ask Spirit to help you get through whatever seems to be troubling you in the moment. Affirm that you have all that you need in this moment. Recognize your fear, and choose another approach that most resembles a loving response.

While you stay open to receiving spiritual love and Jehovah's blessings, take time to re-examine the rules that *you think* you need to follow to receive love. When you stay connected to your spiritual Self you know that you <u>are </u>enough and you <u>have</u> enough. Affirm that you are open to all the love that flows effortlessly through your life. With practice you won't need to try so hard. The law of "Like Attracts Like" operates here. You will draw to you new spiritually connected forms of love when you love yourself and when you stay connected to your spiritual center. Love will appear in many ways and forms even beyond what you imagine. Stay open to all the ways that love may present itself and be ready to receive it.

Become an Open Channel for Love

We do all sorts of crazy things to block out love and then turn around and complain or don't understand why we aren't receiving love. Sometimes we don't welcome in love because the past love we've received has come with all sorts of strings or demands. At other times we've loved deeply and been hurt or disappointed by it. Then we get scared we'll be hurt again and fear opening up to love. Perhaps you've learned to push away love or you don't see that there are other forms of love available to you.

Spiritual Love is readily available to everyone. Love is calling you forth now. Embrace it, welcome it. Rejoice in its beauty, grace and splendor. Celebrate all the ways it shows up in your life.

Here's an example of how I learned to shift through my past programming of love. One day after church when I was having a hard time coming to terms with a relationship ending, my minister suggested I sit with two women who were doing prayer work. I didn't know either of them but thought, "Well, I need something". So I sat and had them offer prayers for me. I had hurt my knee in a softball game a week earlier and was on crutches so they prayed for the healing of my knee. I knew the healing was more for my heart but I let them say prayers for my knee.

Well the funniest thing happened. They kept talking about love and how I needed to welcome that into my life. My first reaction was, "I don't know you." and then to my surprise, I thought, "You don't count, your love doesn't count." Wow what a wake-up call that was for me! Here were two kind women saying prayers over me and offering me their love, and since I didn't know them, I dismissed their love. Here were loving beings offering their healing love to me, and I was rejecting it. I was shocked by how I was pushing away their love. We really can sabotage ourselves in such interesting and profound ways.

After that prayer session I got in my car and just laughed at how ridiculous I had been. I got almost giddy recognizing this important insight into my behavior and thoughts. How many other times had I dismissed love being offered to me because it didn't take the form that I wanted or expected it to take? I knew if I couldn't accept love in the smallest ways it was offered, I'd be missing out on so many other opportunities to experience love (human) and Love (Spirit).

I have since learned to open myself to the various forms that human acts of love and Divine Love manifest in my life. Look for the ways that love presents itself in all the wondrous forms it takes. Think of a typical day for you. What gestures of love, caring, compassion, or support do you receive? Are you aware when you receive it? Do you give thanks when you receive it? Allow the soothing blanket of Love to wrap around you.

The reason we get so tripped up working with Spiritual Love is the Hollywood version we each have about love. We see it as flowers and romance and being swept off our feet. We don't see Love as someone offering to fix our roof, or helping us with homework, or offering to carry our load. You may shut out offers of Love or find yourself too busy to offer your Love in simple ways to others. What a shame we look for love expressed in limited ways. Disentangle the Hollywood version of love and see the numerous ways Love pervades your life.

You've heard the expression, "Be careful what you ask for you'll likely receive it." Well that's certainly true with love. If you had a past relationship where love was demanding, you probably want a love that's not demanding but then find it boring and thus walk away from it. If you want a love that is passionate, you may be overwhelmed by the intensity of it. If you want a love where you feel needed, you will find a love where your partner takes from you continuously or won't be responsible for her actions.

Think of the ways you have wanted to receive love and the ways it has been brought to you. See how you give love in conditional ways.

- *How do you offer love?*
- *When you give love what do you expect in return?*
- *Where do those expectations come from?*
- *Do you get frustrated when you aren't loved in the way that you love others?*

Now think about yourself as a spiritual being—how do you give and receive love at a soul level?

After reading Gay Hendricks' books, *Conscious Living* and *Conscious Loving*, I created an affirmation that I put on my computer. "Thank you God for helping me create and have loving, high vibrational relationships with <u>all</u> the people involved in my life." This affirmation has helped me stay open to all ways I receive love. It helped me remember that I can create loving relationships with anyone I encounter. This shifted my limited view that love came from a few select people or one special person.

Start by simply smiling at someone in a grocery store or while waiting in line. You can practice offering unconditional love to those around you anywhere you are. These situations are good practice ground because there is little danger in doing this, except maybe a quizzical stare in return from a stranger. When you feel ready, offer your love to someone more emotionally close to you. Do an act of kindness not expecting anything in return. Act simply for the joy of giving. Or you can refrain from being critical or complaining when someone does something that annoys you. This too is an act of love.

In the Sufi tradition, there is a practice of the four C's: Refrain from Complaining, Comparing, Criticizing, and Condemning. Try doing this for a week and see how you feel. In all likelihood, you will have a hard time going even a single day without doing one of the four C's. But still keep going the whole week. Notice when you complain, then simply love yourself anyway. Don't add to it by criticizing yourself for being so bad that you can't even go a day without complaining. You likely will find that as you give up these for C's in your day, you'll be a more loving person and feel the joy of Spirit on a more regular basis.

You can try this practice with respect to one person. See if you can refrain from doing one of the four C's with just your boss or a co-worker who particularly annoys you. Make a mental note when you complain or criticize, etc. Start again and see how long you can go without doing it again. Practice this intentionally for a week, and see if you can go an entire day without complaining, criticizing, comparing or condemning someone who usually annoys you.

Then try another week to see if you can refrain from the four C's with more people in your life. Then see if you can go another week doing this with respect to a government official or TV commercial. The object is to go a whole day without complaining, criticizing, comparing or condemning any living being or any event. When you do this you are in the flow of all things accepting them as they are. This practice will help you strengthen your Spiritual Love muscles.

This Sufi practice is one of many spiritual practices that will help you stay connected to your Spiritual Self. Meditations, breath-work, yoga, and daily prayers are all good ways to help you reconnect with your Divine Essence. Affirmations, scripture verses, and mantras are also helpful reminders of God's infinite presence. I have a regular routine of prayers and visualizations every morning and evening to help me find and stay connected to God's Light and Love. One of my morning prayers is known as the Great Invocation. It is found at the end of this chapter. I've added a visualization to go along with it and modified some words to be more universal. This meditation is useful for centering and sending out your Light to the world.

Spreading Love by Staying Connected to Love

You can't feel Spiritual Love and judgment at the same time. They are two opposing energies which don't co-exist at the same time. When you judge yourself or others you send energy of condemnation. Whoever is the target of that condemnation will feel your energy, consciously or not. When you get the urge to judge or condemn, find a way to think of something you love about yourself or that person. God-Love will fill the space occupied by your judging thoughts and the energy will shift. This is important spiritual practice for your own transformation and impacts the world around you.

One of my favorite books is *Peace is Every Step* by Thich Nhat Hanh. It is about being the example of peace that you want to create in the world.

Your life is the journey of peace and love and it is demonstrated by your actions and thoughts. Focus your intention daily to have your life be the peace and love that you wish to create in the world. Sharing love by being a Light for others is essential for these times.

You also can reduce fear by opening your connection to Spiritual Love and sending it towards the object of your fear. Love and fear hold incongruent energy waves. Love dissolves fear. See how energy in a room shifts when you offer love rather than fear. Here's a story I absolutely love to tell to illustrate this process.

Peace Pilgrim was an 80 year-old woman who walked across the country dozens of times talking to people about peace and simply being peace. Once on her journey a truck driver stopped to pick her up. She accepted the ride since she was hot and tired. She sensed right away this man was an angry and dangerous man. Instead of moving into her fears, she simply reached across and touched his hand and said, "I feel so safe being here with you. I know you will take really good care of me." She then proceeded to tell him about her travels and tears started welling up in the man's eyes. He said no one had ever trusted him like that or offered that kind of unconditional love to him before. He said he had stopped with the intention to harm her, but after meeting her he knew he had another purpose. For months after that he was her personal body guard and made sure she was taken care of.

It's amazing what will happen when you open yourself to that form of unconditional love towards others. I had a similar, though somewhat less dramatic, incident when I traveled in India a few years ago. In India it's very common for beggars of all ages to stop you and ask for money. I had traveled to India before and so was prepared for that type of interaction on the street. One day standing on a train platform a man approached me and just stood about a foot away from me. He didn't hold out his hand for money and I wasn't sure exactly why he was staring at me. I decided not to go into my place of fear but to be very intentional about staying in a place of Love.

I closed my eyes and imagined white light surrounding the man and covering him with love and peace. I held that image in my mind for several minutes and sent him Reiki energy as I was holding this vision. After a bit I opened my eyes and he just smiled and walked away. An Indian colleague who was standing next to me saw what happened and was astonished. He asked "what did you do?" I told him the visualization I did and that I sent this man Love energy. My colleague said he wanted to learn how to do it. I laughed and said, "Yes we all need to learn how to do that. The planet would be a whole lot better place if we sent love to others when we are fearful rather than act out of fear."

It was an extraordinary experience for me. It was the first time I intentionally sent unconditional love to someone who I thought was threatening me rather than reacting with fear. It was powerful for me and evidently powerful for the other two men as well. I've since done this in NY City on a subway with a street person who was begging. I did this with street children in India as well and found that the general response of the person receiving the energy is a smile and sometimes laughter. They feel the Love energy they are receiving and appreciate it.

When you open yourself to Love rather than shut down from fear, you shift your energy to experience the situation in an entirely different way. You may still feel fear, and still feel your heart pounding. The key is to be aware in that moment to ask for and draw forth the healing power of Spirit. Taking a more objective, detached view of the situation will help you acknowledge the fear, but not retreat emotionally or defend yourself from a perceived attack. It's a tough but important distinction to feel the fear and at the same time be detached enough emotionally from the situation to shift out of fear and instead offer Divine Light and Spiritual Love. When you can recognize your fear and quickly shift into the abundant Love that is flowing through you, you can serve as a channel for Love in any situation.

You can serve as a channel for Love in any situation.

Not only will you feel physically lighter by filling up with Love and compassion, but you won't feel so anxious or distracted by the fear.

Connecting with your spiritual essence in the midst of daily living allows you to be in the flow of Love. There is incredible peace and harmony in allowing the flow to move effortlessly through you. Life situations emerge that challenge you, but you needn't react or cling to what is happening. You can simply be present to it all, allowing Spirit to flow through you in the moment. When you know that all is happening for a greater purpose, even if you don't see it at the time, there is nothing to do but stay open to the unfolding with Love and inner peace.

Developing "An Attitude of Gratitude"

In the Jewish tradition there is a toast often given at meals—L'Chaim. It means "To Life." The expression simply acknowledges that life is given to us as a gift. Whether we live wisely or foolishly is up to us. I love the quote by Jack London, "It's not the hand you are dealt that counts but how you play your hand." Too many times we look for a better hand to play. We search for the perfect job, the perfect mate, the perfect neighborhood in order to be happy. It is part of our ego-self human nature to strive for more or better. Here's a news flash—if you are not happy with what you have, you'll never be happy with more. And as Caroline Myss reminds us, "Happiness is an inside job."

Developing an attitude of gratitude is a wonderful spiritual practice for staying connected to your soul. It's easy to feel defeated by life's challenges, to feel drained by yet another demanding task. One way to fill up your emotional well is to take stock of all those things that come into your life that help you meet your life tasks. It helps you see that your well is fuller than you might otherwise think. When I give thanks for the people who helped me get through the day or celebrate the things that didn't go wrong, it is a good reminder that I'm being cared for and that I have many blessings.

You've probably found that when you express your gratitude for what you have, many more blessings appear in your life. Get in the practice, if you don't already, to set aside some time in your day when you can give thanks for all the blessings you are receiving. You can do that in the shower, driving to work, as prayers before meals, before you go to bed. It matters <u>that</u> you do it more than when and where. If you can get into a routine of finding things to be grateful for and stopping to acknowledge them, it becomes more woven into your mental and emotional patterning.

The test comes when you can feel gratitude during stressful or difficult situations. Stop in the midst of turmoil to give thanks that this too is a spiritual moment. These times challenge your ability to integrate your spirituality into your daily living. This is where faith comes in—the demonstration of grace not yet seen. Stay open to the flow of Spirit by keeping an attitude of gratitude rather than falling further into your suffering by complaining or criticizing.

Even if you can't possibly see how this painful situation is a blessing, still offer gratitude that Spirit is working through you in a way that will bring you further along in your soul journey. A colleague who survived breast cancer shared this prayer she kept repeating during the course of her treatment, "thank you God for this cancer and what it will reveal to me." Our blessings may not be seen or understood until we have worked through a difficult situation and come out the other side. It also is true that sometimes the best blessing you could receive is not getting what you expected.

Even when things look confusing or scary, or you don't get what you want, stay open to Divine Presence coming through. You often don't know the higher good that is being created. Are you quick to judge what is happening as good or bad? Do you try to plead, to negotiate with God for something better? It is important to see that in the midst of strife or struggle, Love is trying to come through. Love teaches us to keep an open heart, to forgive, to honor, to accept what is rather than stay stuck in fear or shame or anger.

Here's a prayer that I got from Rev. Diane Scribner-Clevenger to stay connected to Source with gratitude:

> *God is my source and therefore I dwell in the midst of Infinite Abundance.*
> *The River of Life never stops flowing through me and out into my world.*
> *I give thanks that Good is coming to me through wonderful and unexpected avenues, blessing me and my world in myriad ways.*
> *I give freely and faithfully into Life with love and gratitude and Life gives back to me with fabulous increase.*
> *Thank you Sweet Spirit.*

Give thanks every day for all those wonderful things that went right in your life that day and for all the blessings big or small that you've experienced. You'll not only notice more of the positive things that happen to you by paying such attention to it; you'll also help create more blessings. As you develop an attitude of gratitude and find joy in the smallest things, you will draw to you other people who have similar energy. As you shift your energy you naturally draw in similar energy. This is the Law of Attraction—**Like Energy Attracts Like Kind**. Pay attention to how it works in your life.

Find ways to remind others of their Light and Love. Take time to make a call or send an email or just put out a thought for someone who might be struggling to let them know you are thinking of them. Give thanks throughout your day or week for those people who offer their gifts to you.

> *If you look to others for fulfillment you will never be truly fulfilled.*
> *If your happiness depends on money you will never be happy with yourself.*
> *Be content with what you have, rejoice in the way things are.*
> *When you realize there is nothing lacking the world belongs to you.*
> -Lao Tzu-

End of Chapter Exercises

Here are three meditations you can use to help you connect to your Source of Light and Love.

1.

Breathe in three slow and steady breaths, feeling the in-breath and out-breath moving through your body. Imagine brushing your worries and fears and putting them into a white sack. In your mind, tie the sack with a golden thread and send it out for Spirit to transform. Release your attachment to those fears and see the sack float out into a radiant light. Know they will be taken care of in Divine Right Order.

Now turn your attention to your day and allow yourself to breathe in peace and harmony. If you think of a challenging situation in your day, ask for and stay open to guidance and clarity. Listen and feel what comes to you. Imagine being a clear and open channel for Love to move through you as you deal with this situation. As you feel more at peace, breathe deeper and let your body fill with Prana, the breath of Life. Feel the stillness, the peace, the centeredness of your soul.

2. Record this to use later or have a friend read this to you:

    I invite you now to close your eyes and take a deep breath:

    Imagine yourself being bathed in love that is soothing, calming, freeing, nurturing. Feel how good it is to have this Love present in your life. Take a deep breath and draw in warm pulses of love and feel it wash over you. You are being held and tenderly caressed.

    Now sink even deeper into this flow of Love coming to you. Every part of your body is taking in this Love and you feel the warmth move through your body, into your cells, your bones, into all your muscles and organs. Know that this Love is always available to you as you open up to your Divine Essence. You can draw in this Love anytime you choose. Just call on this Love to be with you. Welcome and open yourself to receive it.

3. Here is the meditation I use every morning to help me be a channel for peace. I have adapted "The Great Invocation" (attributed to Alice Bailey) with words that are more universal and put visualizations with each stanza.

   Find a quiet time when you can use this meditation. Read each stanza one at a time. First read the imagery and then close your eyes to get it clear in your mind. Feel the image in your body. Then read the words for that stanza and close your eyes again to feel the power of the imagery and the words. Repeat this for each stanza. After you do this for several weeks you'll be able to do the meditation with your eyes closed the entire time, invoking the images as you recite the words.

The Great Invocation

[Imagine yourself sitting as the Buddha, cross legged with your right palm in your lap facing up and your left arm bent with palm facing forward. Imagine a beam of white or gold light coming from the center of your forehead]

From the point of Light within the Mind of God
Let Light stream forth into the minds of all
Let Light return to earth.

[Imagine yourself as the Christ, standing in a field with your hands down at your side facing forward.
Imagine a rose or violet colored beam of light coming from your heart]

From the point of Love within the Heart of God
Let Love stream forth into the hearts of humankind
Let Love return to earth.

[Imagine staring at a glass orb that is reflecting out beams of light in all directions]

From the center where the Will of God is known
Let Purpose guide the little wills of humankind
The Purpose which the Masters know and serve.

[*Imagine sitting or standing in a large circle shoulder to shoulder with people of all races, ages, sizes*]

From the center where the Race of Humankind is known
Let the Plan of Light and Love work out
and may it seal the door where evil dwells.

[*Now breathe deeply and fill your body with peace*]

Let Light and Love and Power
restore the Plan on Earth.

CHAPTER 4

✠

Embracing the Shadow

It doesn't interest me who you know or how you came to be here.
I want to know if you will stand in the center of
the fire with me and not shrink back.

Oriah Mountain Dreamer

Many great myths and stories address darkness in the world. An ancient Greek myth tells of the sin-eater who went from village to village ingesting the demons of the people to purify them. A modern science fiction story tells of a planet where the people all live blissfully and without disease because one of them has been sacrificed, locked in a cave to take on all the illness and evils. That caged person must live in misery so the others can continue to live happily.

In some cultures villages would sacrifice an animal as an offering to the gods to rectify the wrongs that the people had committed. They would often tie objects around the animal before it is killed to symbolically destroy their sins. This is where we get the term scapegoat. One interpretation of the Jesus story is that he represents the universal archetype of both the sin-eater and the scapegoat. He offered his life to release the world of their sins and to purify humanity.

We see evidence of collective scapegoating when we project all our fears onto a person (e.g., Osama bin Laden) or group (immigrants). Some today still believe we will be rid of evil in the world if we defeat or kill that person or group. The Holocaust is an example of societal scapegoating. Some Germans were frustrated by their economic situation after World War I and became convinced that one group of people were responsible for their troubles so set out to eliminate them. People who believe that God is punishing homosexuals by giving them AIDS also are engaged in scapegoating. They are projecting their fears around sexuality and perceived threats to their lifestyle onto a group of people.

When we scapegoat others we don't understand that fear and hatred come from inside our hearts. It's often not "out there" somewhere in a foreign country or embodied by a group of people; the seeds rest in our own hearts. As long as people don't find constructive channels for their fears, pain, or hatred, they will blame problems on others and see some enemy as embodying all the wrongs of the world. The groundwork for ridding the world of terrorism comes in healing pain and hatred, not more violence and killing.

Scapegoating happens in organizations all the time. Someone takes the fall for the collective mistakes. Rarely is corporate corruption or malfeasance the result of one person. Unless people take responsibility for their actions, the problems persist. People may feel good for the time being because the scapegoat has been killed (driven out of the organization etc.) but the problems will remain. Unless the system that perpetuates the problems is fixed there will be another problem and another scapegoat somewhere down the road. The destruction and hurt will be perpetuated. The global economic instability continues because there is no one person or group to blame for the 2008 tumble; numerous institutions contributed by their actions or negligence. The causes are many and wide-spread, with too few people owning responsibility for their mis-steps.

In Jungian terms the shadow represents those qualities we don't want to claim as our own. One great appeal of the Star Wars movies is its classic archetypal depiction of Lightness and Darkness. Luke Skywalker must defeat Darth Vader, his father, representing the dark force within himself. For a new generation, the Harry Potter stories tell a similar tale. Harry must defeat Lord Valdemort, whose dark soul is partly contained within Harry. Lord Valdemort is even referred to as "He who cannot be named", the ultimate shadow title!

Embracing the Shadow

Your shadow elements are those aspects of yourself that you don't acknowledge. Yet to be fully whole and integrated, you must claim or bring your shadow qualities into the open. Continually ignoring your shadow

> _Your shadow elements are those aspects of yourself that you don't acknowledge._

will only result in it coming to the surface when you least expect it or are stressed. I believe September 11, 2001 was just such an incident. It was a wake-up call for Americans to pay attention to how the military industrial complex and financial industries are operating. The following decade brought those institutions into more light.

As I wrote earlier about being a light for others, I also must address what the shadow is and how it is a part of life too. The symbol for Taoism is a circle with two opposing swooshes of black and white representing darkness and light that make up the whole of life. One exists within the other. You cannot know the light without seeing the shadow. Thus the Taoist symbol of the whole of life is a circle with half black and half white areas, each area containing a dot of their opposite color (black on white and white on black).

In some Native American traditions people who are able to work with the shadow elements of others are considered to carry owl medicine. Owls can see through the darkness, seeing those aspects that are hidden from others' sight. Owl medicine is considered very difficult medicine to carry because the medicine man can easily be consumed by others' darkness.

There is tangible suffering in the world. People live terrified in their own homes, perhaps even terrified by relatives or neighbors. How do we embrace the shadow while not getting overwhelmed by the sadness and suffering? For many people, the sadness is too much to bear and they can hardly function. It's not surprising so many people are on anti-depressant, drink or smoke to relieve their pain. Yet the relief of the drug only masks the symptoms.

As you become more awakened, you feel the pulse of life that much more intensely—both the light and the darkness. A few years ago I had a powerful experience grieving the pains of others. I was with a group doing a meditation and I got this image of a lamb being surrounded by wolves. I felt an intense rush of grief wash over me. I sobbed uncontrollably for about 10 minutes. I didn't even know where all the pain was coming from but I got a sense I was grieving for others who could not express such pain. When I finished I felt a bit embarrassed crying in front of the group. But to my surprise many in the group expressed thanks that I cried so hard and openly. It allowed them to release their pain and grieve through my tears. Though it was a pretty exhausting experience, I was glad I could be a channel for that level of grief to be released. Those of you who are highly sensitive, and easily pick up energy or feelings of others, don't be surprised if you experience these types of unexpected or unexplainable emotional swells.

Taking life on life's terms means embracing the shadow and darkness as well as the light. Just as Arjuna didn't want to do battle with his relatives in the epic story of the Bagavad Gita, there are times when you must face the dark side of life that you'd rather not face. The shadow entails those traits, experiences, behaviors or beliefs that are sad, painful or far from praiseworthy. Admitting you can be selfish, self-righteous, judgmental, critical, intolerant etc. is difficult.

Some beliefs and personal qualities may lie hidden or dormant for years without being recognized. Since writing my first book, I tapped into a vein of deep sadness that I didn't even know was there. In order to land on more firm ground, I needed to do some tough, emotionally grueling work to find my wholeness. Working through my darkness has made me more open and compassionate towards others working through their pain.

In one of my workshops, we were discussing the shadow. A participant, who had been through the 12 steps of AA, said that she had an alcoholic friend struggling with his drinking. She shared, "If I can't help him up, I'll help him down." It was her hope that one way or the other her friend will open up to working on his past pain and shadow qualities, what AA calls character defects.

People who have gotten sober say they are thankful for AA groups to provide a safe space and support network for doing their shadow work.

Most likely you won't want to do this work alone. It can be overwhelming. Without some resources or support to do this work, most people won't start. Often people reach their breaking point when the cracks in their facade crumble their self-image of wholeness. Those cracks will continually reappear whether you want them to or not. This is your soul nudging you to move towards healing. Taking the time and setting the intention to address your shadow and past wounds may be the most important work you ever do.

Anger appears routinely at work, at home, with family. It shows up regularly as headlines in the media. Yet fear, jealousy, vulnerability, and woundedness often underlie that anger. The shadow appears most often when people feel threatened. It can come out as being petty, backstabbing, manipulative or intimidating. It may appear in attacking words or emotional games or as self-directed violence of binge eating or drinking. Both physical and emotional attacks create harm. Either way it comes from a place of woundedness that needs to be addressed. Oppression and violence often result from unrecognized woundedness.

I read a few years ago about some men in a sports bar who started giving each other wedgies. It turned into more than juvenile teasing between these men (I don't know how much alcohol played into this situation). Ultimately the one man got really mad and attacked the other man in the parking lot and ended up killing him. How sad, not only that the man was killed but that the man who killed him didn't have enough awareness of his own shadow to know that some deeper wound was being triggered. Instead of backing off and dealing with his own pain, the man took his anger, frustration or pain out on the other man. Not many of us would like having someone physically bothering us, but we can prevent harassment from escalating to physical attacks by being more in touch with our own emotions and hot buttons. It is so unfortunate when people don't stop and reflect when they are feeling hurt. Some people find it difficult acknowledging their pain or vulnerability.

Various support groups provide structured safe environments to acknowledge emotional pain. The ManKind Project (MKP) helps men work through their shadow by having men receive validation from other men in supportive ways. Our American society honors strength over vulnerability, yet there is much strength gained by acknowledging your vulnerabilities. While our culture under-values the benefits of crying or openly showing grief or vulnerability, tears can be so cleansing. Releasing those pent up feelings of anger, disappointment, sadness etc. can help lift heaviness from your heart.

For those who need permission from someone else to claim your vulnerabilities, I officially grant permission for you to deal with your vulnerabilities in the timeliest and most supported way you can.

When you feel tempted to lie, intimidate or manipulate, stop and ask yourself—*Why is this (outcome or behavior) so important to me?* The most common response is "I want this"—whatever <u>this</u> is—love, an object, sex, food, power, money, etc. To uncover your shadow, stop and ask yourself:

*   *What does this _____ represent for me (e.g., power, status, affection)?*
*   *What would happen in my life if I didn't have that?*
*   *How could I still feel whole (loved, important, protected etc.) if I didn't have that?*

Too many times we think we need something external (social accolades, material goods, sex) to affirm who we are when our woundedness is what is preventing us from feeling how we want to feel.

I like the song by David Wilcox about a guy who realizes he must end a relationship. In the song the guy realizes he could keep pouring all the love into his partner's life and it would continue to spill out. Unless his partner fixed the crack in her vessel, she'd never be happy. We need to fix the cracks in our vessel or else all the money, power, praise, status, love etc. in the world will never fill us up. We'll never feel we have enough or are enough to feel content. It not only hurts you in the long run but also those whom you care about (and even hurts those around you whom you don't care about).

Tools for dealing with the Shadow

I've done some powerful shamanic drumming to get in touch with the shadow side. I lead people in these journeys using my shaman drum to guide the visualization of entering into their hidden or unknown self. Imagine entering a cave or tunnel or tree root or some other way down into your own darkness. From there you call forth something that needs healing, whether it's physical healing or emotional healing. When the wound that needs healing is evident, you can call on spirit guides or seek clarity on how to do the healing that needs to be done. It's very powerful to embrace the shadow element and release some of its power.

While I often rely on friends to cheer me up and affirm my Divine Essence, I have learned also to do that for myself. Now when I'm feeling hurt or disappointed I allow my adult loving Self to nurture and support my wounded inner child who needs extra comfort. This may be as simple as telling myself 'It's Okay to feel sad and cry for a while.' Giving yourself permission to be vulnerable, to feel your shadow in a supported way is part of your journey to wholeness.

Here's a prayer you can use as you move through your shadow work:

Spirit of Life and Love, I see the struggle here and feel the pain. Help me with this pain and sorrow. I ask for the pain to be released and the clarity for me to see my next steps. I know all is for the greater good so help me see this experience in the most beneficial way. If there is healing here for me to do, help me with this healing and provide me the strength to address my wounds. I pray to learn whatever lesson is to be learned from this. I claim now that my healing is done and that I no longer need to experience this pain. I call in my greater guides now to assist me in learning and healing. Thank you Divine Wisdom Within (God, Allah, Abba, Yaweh, Great Spirit) for all that is moving through my life at this time for my greater healing and new beginnings.

It takes tremendous amounts of self-awareness, perseverance, courage and patience to look deep within yourself and identify those ways that your ego and woundedness get in the way. Painful as it may be to acknowledge how you create your own suffering and dramas, this awareness is your ticket through the pain. As a soul being of infinite potential, you co-create your reality, both the healing and the perpetuation of pain. You may be embarrassed or discouraged at first as you take responsibility for your woundedness. Yet that's a necessary step in healing and personal transformation.

Your wounds generally play out in your relationship dynamics. That's where you can see how you over-react or misinterpret things according to your own filters and biases. Next time someone really triggers your anger, stop and ask yourself,

* *What is really bothering me?*
* *How is this person mirroring for me something about myself I need to see?*
* *What belief or value (e.g., my security or sense of self) is threatened by this person?*

You may find that you have a wound related to a deeper disappointment, fear, pain, or sadness. I like the Buddhist teaching that 'pain in life is inevitable but suffering is optional'. It is by clinging to what we think *should* happen that we continue to suffer.

You may perpetuate your own pain by clinging to positions in a self-righteous manner trying to prove to yourself and others how right you are. You may defend your position to such an extent that you continue the pain by feeding the wound with your judgments. Working to clear out your 'shoulds' will help you feel less pain. Learn to stop and ask yourself, '*Is it more important to be right or to be at peace?*' Or another question I like to use—'*How can I see this situation differently?*'

I highly recommend Byron Katie's work (www.thework.org) as a method for questioning your beliefs when others trigger your hot buttons. You can find her worksheets on her website that outline four basic questions to help you examine your ways of thinking. Katie's work is based on the premise that our thoughts perpetuate our suffering. When you can challenge and reframe your thoughts about other people or your life circumstances, you can find lasting peace. Her questions are:

1. *Is that true?*
2. *Can you absolutely know that is true?*
3. *How do you react, what happens, when you believe that thought?*
4. *Who would you be without that thought?*

These are powerful questions to help uncover your shadow thoughts, beliefs and feelings that need to be examined. These questions reframe how you interpret other's behavior or situations that *you perceive* to be causing you pain. You'll learn to react differently to others who behave in ways that you don't like.

People often over-react when they have a pain that is triggered. If you have insecurity around money, for instance, and work with someone who uses money as power, you are likely to have a strong emotional response to their behaviors. Your inner wounds serve as a hook that the other person's actions tugs (the proverbial jerking your chain). You'll know when others push your hot buttons by the emotional charge you'll have. Those hot buttons are inside you, they are not about the other person at all. It's up to you to clear out those hot buttons and tend to your wounds. As tempting as it may feel, it's not about fixing the other person; it is about healing your own wounds. Or as they say in Alcoholics Anonymous, "Clean up your own side of the street first."

You may overreact by projecting a previous wounded experience on to a current situation. You also may perceive a threat to be bigger than it really is. You may over react to a threat because your sense of vulnerability triggers you to blow things out of proportion. Next time you catch yourself overreacting or telling yourself a story of how awful things are going to be, examine your story. You'll find greater peace by recognizing when you are creating your own suffering by the thoughts you allow to percolate in your head.

The future is full of potential scenarios. You can focus on the possibility of awfulness or the possibility of everything working out fine. Affirm that the event or issue will unfold as it needs to or that you won't be harmed from it. How many times have you heard some bit of news and immediately thought the worst? Give situations a chance to unfold before you immediately jump to conclusions about how awful something is going to be.

Once you recognize when your shadow elements are triggered or emerge, pay attention to what you do with the feelings or thoughts. One friend uses the phrase "Cancel, cancel" to remove a negative or fearful thought she just had. Another friend uses the expression, "I circle this thought with light". All sorts of thoughts can float through your mind. They are just thoughts. They only carry weight and affect us if we let them. You don't have to obsess over any of them. You can allow them to float by, recognizing your judgments or perceptions of the situation without staying attached to any of those thoughts.

Usually people express their shadow qualities during a time of stress or fear. You can address your concerns by writing down all those worries or beliefs you want to release. Then burn the paper over a candle or in a large bowl. A burning bowl ceremony is very helpful for symbolically releasing fears or old wounds. As part of my morning meditation, I brush my hand over my body and ask that I be released of those things that do not serve my highest good. To physically release the energy collected in your etheric or auric field, use a feather in strokes down your arms and across your body. Similarly you can make a motion with your hands like you are using scissors to cut and release whatever keeps you stuck in fear or does not serve your highest good. Ask that these binds be lifted from you and released into the Spirit realm for transformation. Remember when working with your angel guides, totem animals, or Higher Power, you need only ask to receive assistance.

Here's a prayer you can use or adapt as you need:

> *Mother/Father God (Holy Spirit, Allah, Divine Presence) I pray to release of all those things that are not in my right highest good. Deliver me from that which is not in perfect alignment with the highest plan and purpose for my life. May I be released from all pain, past or present, that holds me back from expressing and experiencing the Divine Light of Love.*

Use whatever prayers or affirmations help you in times of stress when your shadow emerges. Of course a good therapist or support group can also help you move through your shadow. The growth of AA and other support groups as well as women's and men's groups is evidence that more of us are willing to deal with our shadow side. Other people help us recognize our wounds and can provide support for us changing our unhealthy patterns.

Basic View of Humanity

I had an interesting conversation with a woman who was working the polls on Election Day 2004. I realized that we had different political perspectives because we had different views of humanity. From her world view, people were basically wicked and needed to be controlled or forced to change their ways. As I paid attention to her view of humanity, I realized that her political views made sense. I shared that people certainly had the potential for doing horrific things, but that they also had the potential to do tremendous good. This woman clearly believed that evil existed and needed to be defeated or controlled.

An age-old question is why/whether evil exists. Some believe that evil is a quality that exists within people. My own belief is that evil is present or enacted when people disconnect from their Source of Love (Divine Light, Higher Power). Evil is not a quality in and of its self. Just as darkness is the absence of light, evil is the absence of Love.

> *Just as darkness is the absence of light, evil is the absence of Love.*

My experience is that people act for the benefit of others when they come from a place of peace and wholeness in their own heart. Many paths to finding peace and wholeness exist, some involving a savior or invoking a transcendent presence for healing. Other paths such as yoga, psychology, or Buddhist meditation help people find inner peace. Some people can do their healing work purely from their own willpower, others need greater strength and support from a group. People will do their healing work when they are ready to heal.

The stormy winds blow when others are still reacting out of their wounds. The reason this is called 'shadow' work is that people are not aware of their pain, they don't see it. Destruction and suffering happen from people reacting out of their woundedness. Yet pain can be a useful force to recognize wounds or old patterns that need to be released. If adequately addressed, pain can be an important lens for awareness to change old patterns so that new healthy ways can be created. Destruction often is needed for rebirth, as in the Hindu representation of Shiva, the Destroyer or Transformer.

Several people I know have done peace work in Israel. They share stories of powerful healing that occurs when people sit down to listen to each other's experiences of suffering. From their shared stories of pain and suffering new understanding emerges between the different parties. What usually becomes clear is that regardless of their religion or ethnic group, they all want the same thing for their families. They all want peace, safety, health and happiness for themselves and their loved ones. We all want this. What gets in the way are our interpretations and beliefs about what others are doing. By focusing so much on what the "other" is doing to prevent peace, we fail to see how we are also blocking peace from happening for ourselves and others.

The Shadow Brings a Gift

Even as you work through your pain, you will always have a shadow side. You can't get rid of your shadow side, but you can admit you have it and learn to understand when and how it appears in your life. Being human involves a range of emotions and behaviors that serve to protect us. Our human brain still contains the reptilian processing of fight or flight. It's only the 'newer' neo-cortex that allows us to make conscious decisions that move us to our next level of healing and growth. As you embrace your shadow you can learn how it serves you in some circumstances.

I'm reminded of a parable of a small boy who was under the tutelage of a Sage. The boy's job was to deliver two large clay pots of water to the Sage at the beginning and end of each day. The Sage spent the day in meditation at the top of a hill so the boy had a big climb to deliver the heavy pots of water. The boy was able to balance the handles of the pots on the ends of a long a stick and carry the stick over his shoulder. He had to walk very slowly to keep the pots balanced and not spill the water as he climbed the hill.

One day the boy was in a hurry, not watching his steps as he walked, and tripped on a stone. One of the pots hit a rock and made a small crack in the clay so that water slowly dripped out as he walked. He hoped the Sage wouldn't notice the crack or notice that there was less water than usual. After the boy delivered the water he quickly ran down the hill afraid to speak or even look at the Sage.

Several days passed by with the boy not saying anything to the Sage about the crack. He feared the Sage would reprimand him for being so careless. Finally, the guilt of not admitting his error was too great and the next morning after he delivered the water, the boy threw himself at the Sage's feet pleading for mercy.

The Sage had the boy look at the path he had been climbing over the past days. The boy had been so consumed by his fear of being punished that he had not been paying attention to the path he was walking. Now as the boy saw the path he cried in surprised, "Master, those flowers, where did they come from?" The sage smiled. "All this time you have been feeding water to the wild flower seeds on the path. You focused on the crack in the pot, not on the water that was helping the flowers. Often we don't see the good that comes from our falls. Go now and enjoy the flowers. You can fix the crack and then later water the flowers if you like them."

I like this story for two reasons. One is that we often get so consumed with covering up our mistakes or running from our character flaws that we fail to see the gift it brings. Each shadow quality has within it a gift that you can use at various times in your life. There may be times when it is useful to be impatient, pushy, radiant or talented. You can uncover the gold in your shadow and use it to your advantage.

The other reason I like this story is that there are always 'crack pots' in our life. Some people have characteristics that drive us crazy. However, if you take the time to look for the gold in their 'cracks', you may find that the quality that most bothers you either tells you something about yourself or has a unique purpose or benefit. Look for the cracks in others and yourself for what the gift may be.

Once you become aware of your shadow and its triggers and hooks, you can retrieve the gift of the shadow. You'll see what the shadow side has to teach you. How have your fears or shadow qualities helped you in some way? You gain strength from your vulnerability by dealing with your shadow.

People develop great defensive mechanisms like humor or intuitive powers. Others escape their wounds by throwing themselves into books and thus become avid readers or very scholarly people. Some people are highly creative and use art or music as an outlet for their shadow experiences.

Your shadow characteristics, those you believe need to stay hidden, can serve a useful purpose. You benefit from uncovering your shadow and bringing it to light. In so doing you can discover the gift of those qualities.

Another way to retrieve the gift of the shadow is to closely examine what's being stirred inside you when you feel intense sadness. Going deeper into your grief rather than running from it allows you to uncover the source of the sadness. The gift will come in finding a deeper level of love, support, acceptance or forgiveness for that source of sadness. Moving into grief often allows you to see something that you treasure, something precious that you want to preserve.

Joanna Macy does powerful workshops getting people in touch with their own despair. Often despair masks deeper feelings of love for the thing that you treasure, whether it is a loved one, yourself, the environment, or other fragile souls. Yet as you move through this sadness you are able to retrieve the gift, such as a new insight, forgiveness, or greater compassion for others.

A friend of mine said that when her oldest son was preparing for college she got incredibly sad. The night before he left she cried for four hours. It was a deep grieving and she couldn't understand why she was crying so hard. After she started journaling to calm down, she realized that few families she knew were closer to their children after they left for college. She finally was able to pinpoint where her sadness was coming from. She didn't want to lose the closeness with her son yet she believed that was an inevitable part of his growing up process. The gift from her grief was finding ways to deepen her connection with her son even if it took a different form than what it had been. She shared that now even though she's not involved in his daily life, she and he connect on a richer level as adults.

Many times the shadow reflects the other side of a feature about us that is positive. You may be highly motivated or driven to achieve. This can be useful in helping propel you in your career. However, if that motivation comes from a wound such as being told when you were younger that you'd never amount to anything, you'll react from that wound. Your feeling of self worth will only come when you feel you've achieved some level of acknowledgement. We've certainly seen this to the extreme with people so driven to achieve that they'll do anything to succeed, even if it means destroying other people's lives. Perhaps you keep striving to compensate for feeling inferior. This is a trap unless you do the healing that is needed to work through your feelings of inferiority. You can strive your entire life and not feel you've accomplished enough or proven yourself enough. People become workaholics to prove how worthy or competent they are, yet never feel good enough. They continue to run like a gerbil on a wheel but never feel content.

Mirroring the Darkness

When you get irritated with someone ask yourself, "When have I done that too?" I like leading the following exercise with groups who are learning about the shadow. Take a piece of paper and divide it into three columns. Then close your eyes and think of someone you have a hard time being around, someone who generally triggers a hot button for you, or who generally gets you irritated or uncomfortable.

Bring to mind this person clearly and a situation when you were bothered by something they did. Once you have this person and situation clearly in mind, on the left column of your paper, write down all the qualities about this person you don't like.

Review this list. For each quality in the left hand column, write down in the middle column the words "just like me". Write this phrase all the way down the middle column for each quality of the other you identified. Then in the right hand column, for each quality you don't like in the other, write down a behavior or instance when you also acted that way or exhibited the quality just like the other person.

Rather than staying stuck in a place of anger or frustration with someone who really ticks you off, use their behavior or qualities to examine how you have those as well. Participants in my workshop have been astonished at what they discover from this exercise. They see that the things that most bother them about someone else are aspects of themselves they haven't recognized or don't want to admit that they have.

This mirroring experience happens most readily when you are dealing with family members. Those characteristics of your parents or siblings that really irritate you are generally ones you've developed as well. It does no good to condemn your parents or siblings for your unhealthy aspects that need to change. In fact the reverse is what is needed. When you are willing to change aspects that you've learned from them, you'll feel more whole yourself. From this place of wholeness you'll be able to act in more healthy ways when you are with them. This change almost always results in a shift in others. The dance of family means that as one person changes steps, the others have to change steps too. Even if a family member doesn't ever change, the beauty is that when you learn to make peace with yourself, you are better able to make peace with others.

Even if the other person who triggers your hot button doesn't change, you still have the opportunity to claim your shadow behaviors and move to a place of acceptance and compassion. It will help ease your heart regardless of whether the other person changes. From that place of calm and compassionate heart, you are able to *be* the peace that you wish to create around you.

There are some great books about paying attention to how others mirror for us what we most need to learn, both in positive forms and in challenging forms. Debbie Ford's book, *Dark Side of the Light Chasers,* is an excellent introduction to this topic. She provides numerous examples and visualizations of how to see that others mirror for us those qualities that we don't want to admit we have. When you are frustrated by someone being dishonest, take stock of the times you have not been honest. When someone beats around the bush and doesn't say what he wants or needs, think of the last time you also didn't ask for what you wanted.

When you see someone being bossy, impatient, controlling or irritable, do you get into a place of blaming and judging or do you honor the fact that she is where she needs to be? As a soul awakened being, remember that you are dealing with your stuff the best way you can, and *so is everyone else.* Just as you've had times of being uncomfortable, unhappy or frustrated, recognize when others are in that place too. Instead of judging, blaming or criticizing others who don't behave as you would like, learn acceptance of them by remembering that you too react in ways that are unhealthy or disturbing for others.

Having said that, some people always seem to hang on to their misery. You can either affirm them being in a place of misery and wish them well moving through their dramas, or you can get hooked into their drama and become another actor in it. It's really easy for people who are caring and nurturing to want to help someone in distress. Instead of getting caught in their drama, you can acknowledge their struggle and affirm their strengths, helping them see that they have the power to attend to their own wounds. It's really tempting to fall into the co-dependent trap and take on the role of savior for others rather than help them learn to save themselves. Learning how <u>not</u> to take responsibility for others' dramas is tough for many people who want to be compassionate and caring.

Listening empathically to what is going on for the other person without jumping in to give advice or fix their life for them may be your best approach. Maybe all that is needed is to listen to them and hold the space for them to vent or cry. Perhaps all they need is for someone to accept them in their struggle without judgment or fixing their problems. Letting someone know you have confidence in their ability to work through their struggle when they are ready to deal with it may be the best act of encouragement and love you can offer them. Allow them to work through their struggles in the way and timing that they need to. You can pray that they find their way and affirm their Divine Essence even when they can't see it in themselves.

End of Chapter Exercises

Think of a time when someone pushed your hot buttons or really set you off. What emotion, value or belief was being triggered for you? Look carefully at this discomfort and find the deeper wound (it may be something around security, feeling a need to be right, feeling a lack of power or control, etc.). Write about this incident below.

<u>Situation:</u>

Feel the emotions that were triggered. How do you feel them in your body? Does your energy level drop when you recall this incident? Get in touch with those feelings. See if you can identify what need you have that's not being met.

Write down your feelings and needs here:

I. Processing Questions:

1. What messages come up for you around this situation? Are there any "shoulds" playing in your head? (messages about what you or the other should be doing)

2. What qualities are the people in this situation mirroring aspects of yourself that you don't like or would like to change in yourself?

3. In what ways have these same qualities been helpful to you in the past?

List ways that your shadow qualities in this situation could be useful or harmful to you.

II. From the situation above, choose those wounds or beliefs that you are ready to release. Bring them clearly to mind as you do the following visualization.

Imagine that the wounds, messages, hooks you want to release are falling from your body to the ground. Now watch them being swept onto a huge blanket on the ground near you. All your old baggage that you want to clear out is being swept onto the blanket. The blanket is large enough to hold all those aspects of you that you no longer want to stay attached to. Imagine taking the corners of the blanket, pull them together and tie them securely with a gold cord.

Call forth a guide in any form to carry this blanket off to be transformed and cleared. Watch your guide carry the blanket off in the distance. As the blanket is being carried away, offer thanks for your awareness of any healing you've needed to do. Thank Spirit for working with you to release those things and for clearing you of whatever weight you have been carrying. Know that you can release these or other wounds in the future whenever you are ready.

CHAPTER 5

✵

Conscious Evolution

If you seek enlightenment outside yourself, any
discipline or good deed will be meaningless.
For example, a poor man cannot earn a
penny just by counting his neighbor's wealth,
even if he does so night and day.

Nichiren

There is a great paradigm shift taking place. More and more people are awakening to their soul journey. The success of the books by Caroline Myss, James Hillman, Thomas Moore and others show that many people are yearning to understand their life from a soul perspective. You are reading this book as proof. As you pay attention to your soul journey and the soul contracts you came to fulfill, you understand why you are born into this life. In the first chapter I spoke of your Learning Agreement. Soul contracts are agreements you made when you entered this physical plane. Those agreements are around your work, your relationships, your health, your finances etc. You consciously evolve as you work through your soul contracts, guided by a Higher Power through your human experiences.

The movie "The Matrix" is a good allegory for seeing through the illusions of the world. As you see the matrix, which in this case is the spiritual unfolding taking place, you'll better understand the events in your life. The key is not to get too hung up on your life conditions as they appear. *You are not your life situation*, you are much bigger than that. Feel the truth of this. Know it, understand it.

Once you fully grasp that you are more expansive than your life conditions, you see through the matrix of <u>what is</u> to a whole new view of your life. Your life conditions are temporal events that can drag you down or buoy you up. Either way, they are merely scenes of your life play. You are an infinite creative being. Your life is positive potential ready to be fulfilled. Your mission, should you choose to accept it, is to learn to move through your life events with greater awareness, ease and joy.

Every major event or decision that happens during your life (and some seemingly minor encounters) supports your soul journey. The "matrix" to see through is that your life conditions are merely the props and plot twists in a gigantic play involving all of us on the planet. Each actor affects everyone else's part. Don't respond to the props as defining who you are and your ultimate reality. See the play for what it is—fulfillment of soul contracts and props for your soul progression. You don't need to stay engaged in the act longer than it needs to go on. You don't need to give power to the props longer than their purpose is served. Sex, attention, money, status, power, relationships, jobs are all props that aid you in your soul's journey. How you use them is up to you.

I love this Buddhist story that illustrates how hard it can be to see 'the matrix' in certain life events. A Buddhist initiate entered the meditation hall and saw his guru weeping uncontrollably. The initiate, feeling great compassion, went to his teacher and asked what was wrong. The master said that he found out that his son had just been killed. The student sat for a while in silence taking in this news. With some hesitancy, the initiate asked his teacher, "You have always taught us that this life is illusion, and not to be attached to earthly matters. Why then are you sobbing?" The teacher looked up through his tears, and with a wry smile said, "Some illusions are harder to see through than others."

You can see past your daily life experiences for the bigger lessons, despite the challenging situation in front of you. What most frequently prevents us from moving smoothly through our soul journey is that we get attached to daily physical experiences. Those attachments, usually coming from fear or ego, are a veil that prevents us from seeing the greater unfolding. To remove the veil, recognize your human based judgments of what "should" be happening.

Conscious evolution entails not only being aware of your judgments, but also releasing your attachments to those judgments. When you learn that your judgments keep you stuck in old thought patterns, you will be able to step into the abundant opportunities for joy and peace. You are so much greater than your judgments. Your Divine Essence is far more expansive that your small ego-self recognizes.

When you act in ways that are disharmonious with your Divine Essence, use it as a learning experience. You have to go through experiences to learn not only how you <u>want </u>to be and act, but also how you <u>don't want</u> to be or act. If you can see the negative effects of your actions, the pain and disharmony you create, you can shift gears and choose a different approach the next time. This is why it's important to understand how your shadow shows up. Don't beat yourself up with more self-judgments when you act in a way that is not in harmony with your Divine Essence.

You are called now to open up, clear out, and re-align yourself—mentally, emotionally, physically and spiritually. This clearing and opening process may feel turbulent or painful at times. It is all for the purpose of your awakening to consciously evolve. As you move through those turbulent times you come out the other side dancing with the Universe.

4th and 5th Dimensional Beings

Now is the time to consciously evolve from a 3rd dimensional being, focused only on the material, physical world, to a 4th dimensional being, guided by Spirit and able to access other realms of consciousness. This evolution takes both awareness and practice. You'll consciously evolve by moving through your experiences aligned with your Divine Essence. Your experiences and lessons may be to help others learn unconditional love, to give and receive unconditional love, to forgive yourself or others, and/or to be more compassionate in the face of fear, danger and destruction. The specific codes that reveal the 'matrix' of your soul journey come from varied experiences.

Azurae Windwalker, a Shamanic healer and teacher, explains that we are in a window of time when conscious evolution can be accelerated. The next step in your conscious evolution is to grow into a 4ᵗʰ dimensional soul being. It is not a coincidence that you have been drawn to this book or other resources now. You've gained awareness of yourself as a soul being.

Your life may seem topsy-turvy during certain periods as you make the necessary changes to advance to a 4ᵗʰ dimensional being. It's all part of your clearing, healing and learning process to shift into another dimension of your conscious awareness. To move through your shifts and the alignment with the earth vibrations, remember that you are <u>always</u> One with the Source of your Being. Hold your conscious intentions to be a channel for Universal Creative Energy. Think and act connected to that Consciousness and you will consciously evolve.

Here are some characteristics of 4ᵗʰ Dimensional beings. See how many of these you are experiencing on a daily basis.

> ➢ Greater sensitivity to energy of other people or physical places
> ➢ Greater Intuition and Insights into life events
> ➢ Easily receive messages from guides (Angels, Elementals, Totem Animals, Ascended Masters etc.)
> ➢ Greater connection to non-physical realms in your awakened consciousness
> ➢ More vivid dreams and lucid dreaming
> ➢ Developed skills in clairvoyance, clairaudience, and other ESP gifts
> ➢ More frequent premonitions or greater prescience (sense of knowing what will happen)
> ➢ Developed divination skills such as dowsing, muscle testing, coning, or use of pendulums
> ➢ Cleared blocks of all seven chakras, etheric fields, and past life traumas
> ➢ Greater flow of energy for healing such as Reiki, Healing Touch, or Energy Medicine

If you experience or use most of these characteristics, you are already operating as a 4th Dimensional being. You are here to offer your gifts and skills for the healing of others on this planet. You are called now to do this more intentionally in support of the alignment and attunement of all sentient beings on the planet. Thanks to Machaelle Small Wright, Peter Calhoun, Wayne Dyer, Deepak Chopra, Esther Hicks, Raymond Grace, and many others who offer their awareness and knowledge, more of us are learning these skills. Your personal awareness and conscious evolution benefits us all.

> *Once you shift into 4th dimensional consciousness, you won't go back to your previously un-awakened state.*

Once you shift into 4th dimensional consciousness, you won't go back to your previously un-awakened state. You may move back and forth between a 3rd and 4th dimensional states in various situations. Yet you will remain aware when you are operating out of each dimension and what you need to do to move back into your 4th dimensional state. As you consciously evolve into more complete 4th dimensional living, the pain and confusion of 3rd dimensional living eases and you ride the current of Universal Energy more smoothly.

Masters such as Sathya Sai Baba, Amma, and Meher Baba have evolved into 5th Dimensional beings. Some of you may have experienced the presence of these Masters. They held in their consciousness the truth of their being—that they are a channel of Consciousness. Regardless of whether you have only fleeting glimpses or can hold that level of Consciousness for a few hours this is the direction where we are all evolving.

These unique Masters have attained the state of Consciousness that is evident in 5th Dimensional Beings. These beings can transcend the human physical needs of water, food, heat etc. They are able to stay in God-Consciousness and regulate their autonomic system to maintain body functions. Yogis and Masters throughout the ages have done this, as have monks and mystics in more modern times. While you may not feel called to progress to 5th Dimensional God-Consciousness, you will more frequently be a powerful channel and presence of Love as you shift to a 4th Dimensional Being.

Harmonic Vibrational Match

Our physical world is a finely tuned, highly charged world of energy fields and thought patterns. We can measure these energy fields and vibrational patterns by various machines in Herz or other units of measure, just as we can measure sound or light waves. As you raise your energy to the higher frequencies, your physical world changes accordingly. Conversely as the earth vibrations shift, your physical body and life experiences reflect the effects of those planetary shifts. We are more entrained to the earth energy than many realize.

Your energy field is in harmonic resonance with the planet and affects those around you. As you clear your energy fields from blocks caused by old patterns of thinking and behaving or past traumas, you draw in energy of higher vibrations and move more easily in the world. Because Creation is unlimited and unbounded you have that powerful potential in you as well. As you raise your vibrational energy closer to the vibrational frequency of Universal Consciousness, you experience abundant free flow of that Divine-Sourced Energy. The cycles of life, the ebbs and flows, will continue, and you learn to ride these currents rather than struggle against them.

The degree to which you are open to receiving Source and letting it channel through you, is the degree to which you can consciously transform and manifest things in the physical world. All great shamans and energy healers know this. The key is to get out of your own way and allow that Energy to flow through you. Transformational Empowerment$_{TM}$, described in the last chapter, will help you use energy flow more readily for manifesting and co-creation.

You consciously co-create and evolve by understanding how to be in harmonic vibrational attunement with what you desire to experience. Many yogis and master teachers talk about this. Jesus instructs in John 14:12, "The works that I do shall ye do also: and greater works than these shall ye do." What he and others knew was that when we approach Universal Consciousness (the highest form of vibrational frequency) the physical world is merely our playground.

As outlined in the Chapter 2 discussion of matter and energy, life is a continual flow of energy; it is always pulsing and always changing form. As you make shifts in consciousness, you vibrate energetically with the Universal pulse. As you release your blocks and move through your fears, you experience shifts in your energy levels. The Universal Flow of Energy is all around you. Your conscious evolution allows you to ride the waves of your own and others' emotions with better skill and attention. Set the intention and the Universe responds. Kawabunga—surf's up!

For those of you just beginning this path, it may not seem like you are consciously connecting to your soul experiences. As you learn to use your Energy more intentionally for your own or others' growth and benefit, you'll draw to you the right perfect experiences. Likewise, you will become more intentional about not allowing certain experiences, stepping away from dramas and victim consciousness. Taking care of yourself physically, mentally and emotionally is essential for this journey of conscious evolution.

For those of you practiced in this process, you know how to consciously co-create with others who are awakened. You are more skilled and aware daily of your soul nudges and contracts. You know when to stay out of other people's dramas. If you choose to enter into a situation that is challenging for you energetically or emotionally, remember to surround yourself with Light and affirm protection of Spirit. Visualize a shield or bubble that blocks others' harmful energy and ground yourself in these situations. Disconnect any chords to people or things that you do not wish to enter your energy field. Conscious co-creation with Spirit always includes asking that the right highest good be done for all involved.

> *Conscious co-creation with Spirit always includes asking that the right highest good be done for all involved.*

As you consciously evolve into a 4th dimensional being, your daily living will reflect your growing awareness. The more you stay in a place of gratitude and acceptance of all that you experience, the more you will be an abundant channel of God-Sourced Energy. See the beauty of this game? You'll find that life flows more easefully and you move through challenges more quickly. You'll meet other 4th Dimensional beings and revel in the joy of the treasures they bring. Life becomes more of a dance than a struggle.

Conscious co-creators know they can experience life as a playground for joy, love and healing. Your intentions and vibrational energy pull in those events or situations that match your frequency. Decide when and which way you want to move with the beat of the Universe. Remember, you are NOT alone in your journey.

One final point here, while you are a conscious co-creator, so is everyone else. There is the proverbial "primordial soup" of energy flowing around you. The energy that flows from you and around you is constantly stirring and shifting. Important note—Free Will Always Prevails. You can't determine other people's behavior. Your soul journey brings you what you need for your highest experience. How others act or react is not in your control, nor your work to do. That's why we call this work conscious co-creation.

You choose when and how to hold the vibrational pattern that you need in any situation. Sometimes you can hold a higher vibration than at others times. Don't judge yourself as to whether you are vibrating high "enough" or not. No judgment is necessary; judging likely will drop your vibration. The point is to be the best Light you can be at any moment. All the rest of the pieces will fall into place as is necessary. As conscious co-creator you are not the conductor, rather one player of an instrument in the band.

And so the beat goes on.

> *"Quiet the outgoing mental restlessness and turn the mind within. Harmonize your thoughts and desires with the all-fulfilling realities you already posses in your soul. Then you will see the underlying harmony in your life and in all nature."* Yogananda

Managing the Flow and Attachments

One of the best illustrations of life with attachments is the story of how monkeys get trapped. Monkey hunters set up a banana or other favorite food in a cage for a monkey to grab. The monkey can put its hand through the bars and get the food. Once it grabs the food, the monkey can't get its hand out of the bars if it still keeps holding the food. By making a fist the monkey's hand is too big to fit back through the bars. So the monkey will sit there, holding on to the food, until it is caught. It refuses to let go of the food, even to the point of starvation, rather than release it and be free. How often have we done that to ourselves—held on to something way past the time that it was useful for us?

You don't need to <u>cling</u> to get what is in your highest good. The sweet flow of Source is infinite. You simply focus your attention on what is true to your soul journey and allow the next right highest good to emerge. Just as the monkey clings, attachments will get you into trouble every time. The hardest ones to release are those things that tempt you and you feel you must have to be happy.

Conversely, those things that you feel you must defeat are also attachments when you have judgments of how things 'should' be rather than accepting how they are. Grabbing <u>or</u> destroying both stop the flow of Universal Energy. The Flow is ever present, so let go of your attachments to a specific outcome or specific behavior. The more you resonate with the Universal Flow, the greater you experience the rhythm of life as it is.

Perhaps you are wondering if fear plays any role in conscious evolution. Fear can be a good wake up call to get your attention, so don't completely dismiss feelings of fear when they arise. As mentioned in the chapter on

Shadow, go into the fear and see what is being shown. The key is to not stay attached to the fear or its source. Fear leads to further pain or destruction when it becomes a way to control others or get what you want.

Here's a good clue for your soul journey—*That which most tempts you or most tests you is what you need to closely examine and probably shift.* Next time you feel yourself getting an emotional charge from someone or some situation (either a positive or negative emotional response) it's a nudge to pay attention to the situation. Stop and ask yourself—*"What do I need to see more clearly here? How can I understand what my soul lesson is in this situation?"*

Temptation tells us what our hooks are—money, affection, power, status, security, intimacy, etc. People can obsess or crave these things to the extreme of addiction. If your wholeness and meaning is dependent upon some hook, you will do whatever it takes to get the fix. When you feel an intense desire that seems to rattle you to your core, stop and pay attention. What does this situation show you about what is meaningful or true to your inner being? The hook gets attached to your ego and cravings. Go deeper and determine—*Who would I be without these things? How can I feel complete even if this wasn't in my life?* You may need to experience the hook or loss thereof to know what your soul needs for its clearing and progression.

When you align with the Universal Flow of Life you feel complete. Jobs can come and go, people can come and go, teachers and heroes come and go. Still you stay grounded through the changes. Many of you have already experienced profound joy, love, happiness and peace as you've cleared your gunk and receive this Flow. Halelu Yah! Alhamdulillah!

Social Change through Conscious Evolution

Our conscious evolution expands when we remember that there is no enemy, no us vs. them—only One, an interdependent all. When you perceive there is an enemy, a person or institution, that needs to be changed or eliminated because "they" are wrong, you have lost connection to

Source. Seeing life situations from a soul perspective, you know there are just actions and consequences. These either promote conscious evolution or delay it. As you understand that what occurs is for your own or another's conscious evolution, your role becomes more clear. Those of you who are 4th dimensional teachers and masters have learned to <u>be love</u> despite the circumstances or events happening.

Some of you may be challenged when you are fighting for something as noble as peace or the love of a child. It's not only your actions that create change, it also is the energy and intention that you have. If you are standing up for yourself by pointing out how wrong or bad someone else is, you lower your own and their vibration and have not created a net positive situation. The age-old view of fighting and winning—'I can only win if the other loses' is over.

Conscious evolution is no longer about winning or losing but affirming the right highest good for all parties and living in alignment with your Divine Essence. Gandhi's basis for non-violence was Satyagraha, meaning "firmness of truth". Rather than speak the truth of your ego, your awakened consciousness resonates with a much more powerful energy of Universal Consciousness. You then stand as witness and bring the universal flow of Source-Energy to your life situations.

As you shift into a 4th dimensional being, you'll remember to send healing, loving prayers and not get thrown off by the illusion of how things appear. By staying connected to the healing and the love rather than the fear and sadness, you raise the vibrational frequency of the situation. As Martin Luther King Jr. wrote, "The non-violent approach does not immediately change the heart of the oppressor. It first does something to the heart and souls of those committed to non-violence." Be the peace that you wish to see in the world, no matter how disharmonious the situation appears.

The greater your ability to move past your initial human reaction, and stay focused on your Higher Power in that moment, the more healing, love and compassion you can offer for the situation. There is a Buddhist phrase—

"May all beings be well, may all beings be happy. Peace, Peace, Peace." I have found this phrase helpful to shift my energy towards peace when I'm feeling challenged or frustrated.

Think of a global situation where you want to ignite the Universal Flow.

Over the next week take 10 minutes a day to visualize harmony, healing, and nurturing being sent to that situation. Visualize the people or place (earth, sky, water, trees, animals) opening and receiving unlimited Universal Energy. Affirm that they are connecting to their Higher Power and operating from a place of love and compassion. Send them your peaceful energy and see all the people involved welcoming and receiving this influx of love and peace, remembering that we all evolve together.

This type of social action provides an opportunity to be a channel of the Universal Flow of Energy. As St. Francis said "make me a channel for your peace." Done in a group with others who are open to bringing in this Universal Flow, the energy becomes more focused and powerful. Here's a wonderful story to illustrate this.

A good friend shared a story of her mom's minister who was doing work in Central America. The minister was building schools in an area where a civil war was brewing. One day while riding his bike to a neighboring village to get supplies, the minister stopped in his tracks. On the road ahead of him were men carrying guns. They were guerillas who had invaded the area. The minister was terrified so started to pray for protection. The guerillas looked at him angrily as he stepped off his bike and walked past them. He just kept praying they wouldn't attack him.

Later on his way home, he ran into these same men, only this time they were more relaxed. One man shouted in Spanish, 'hey gringo. Good thing you were with those 10 soldiers last time or we would have killed you'. The minister thought he had not translated correctly what the man said, but didn't bother to stop and get clarification. The minister just kept going on his bike.

Upon returning home from his mission trip, the minister explained this story to a group of parishioners. Several men in the room gasped and looked around. The minister saw their reaction and asked what they thought. One man spoke up and asked, "Do you remember what day that was?" The minister thought and then recalled the date. The men gasped or laughed. Another man replied, "We were in our prayer meeting that day and felt you needed help. So we all visualized you doing your work safely and prayed for your safe return home." The minister asked how many were in the group that day. The man replied, "There were 10 of us."

Conflicts can be stopped by physical force or by changing thought patterns. The next phase of our evolution is to move away from thinking that the physical world only operates by what can be manipulated and measured. As described earlier, physics is now showing us that events occur across space and time due to shifts of energy fields. Our thoughts and intentions literally change our energy fields and then our life circumstances. Conscious creation is the next frontier in human evolution. The physical sciences are only beginning to demonstrate the non-physical realm of intention and consciousness.

Take time in the next week to visualize a relationship that you want to improve.

> *Visualize how you want to offer love and receive love in this relationship. Visualize yourself as being a loving person who radiates compassion, peace, and harmony no matter what the other person does or says. Affirm that you access infinite abundant Love and share it freely with all those you encounter. Focus on being an expression of love, joy, and gratitude. Know that others involved are also doing their best and highest good.*

At the fifth anniversary of the September 11th attack, a friend of mine offered a prayer for peace and healing globally. I've modified it somewhat below with her permission:

Divine Healer, Protector, Source of ALL that is, we consciously direct your Power and your Light to support a new way for humankind and the awakening on Earth.

We hold this vision:

Where there is grief and emptiness, Let there be Comfort and Hope

Where there is anger and hatred, Let there be Forgiveness and Acceptance

Where there is dis-ease of mind, body and spirit, Let there be Healing and Harmony.

Where there is war or thoughts of war and retribution, Let there be a Tide of Desire for Peaceful Solutions.

Where greed and ego rule, Let the Voice of Spirit and Oneness be Heard and Heeded.

We hold Compassionate Strength, Peace, Prosperity and Harmonious Freedom as our Template from this moment forward.

With great gratitude we rejoice that IT IS SO

Penny Prentice Best

Meeting Needs with God as Your Foundation

The Law of Allowance is the mechanism by which the Universal Flow of Energy operates. Rather than feeling you must force something to happen or submit and feel victimized, you simply allow the Universal Flow to come to you and through you. All your needs will be met in time as you stay connected to this Flow.

Most people who have taken a basic psychology course or management seminar are familiar with Maslow's needs hierarchy. Maslow outlined the progression of human needs that had to be met before one could move on to higher level needs. According to Maslow people who find a deep sense of purpose and bring their unique talents to the world are referred to as self-actualizers. He postulated that only about 10% of the population would achieve self-actualization.

In Maslow's framework, people won't get to higher order needs unless all their lower order needs are met—safety, housing, food, social connections, and lastly self-esteem. Only at that point will people be able to reach a level of greater self-knowledge and larger purpose of their life to become self-actualized.

We are at a stage of human evolution where a vast majority of people can achieve this state of self-actualization. As more people awaken to their soul journey they will strive for self-actualization and 4th Dimensional living.

Maslow's hierarchy makes sense for 3rd dimensional beings. However, as you understand that you live as a spiritual being in a material realm, you meet your needs in a whole new way. Here is another framework to use for conscious evolution.

How are your daily experiences different when you start from the foundation that you are a Spiritual being always connected to the Universal Flow? The fundamental need you must meet is to stay open to receive that Source continually in your life. You flourish when you allow the Universal Flow effortlessly to move through you. When you shut off this Flow you feel lack, pain, or disappointment. Does this sound familiar?

Meeting other needs such as food, housing, friendships, and self-esteem come from this Universal Energy. Though these material needs are in fact necessary for you to move through the physical world, they aren't <u>why you are here</u>! That's a pretty radical idea, yet worth considering. Indeed an important part of conscious evolution is to fully understand how your physical living supports your soul journey.

What if your connection to Source were the most important and fundamental need to tend to and nurture? What if you could change how open you are to receiving the continual flow of energy and abundant grace? Would your life look and feel different? Absolutely!

You wouldn't need to struggle so hard to earn, find, or keep those things of the material plane that seem so illusive or challenging. Jobs could come and go and you'd have confidence that all is in Divine Right Order.

Relationships could end and you'd know that you were experiencing exactly what was needed for your right highest good. Children could disobey you and you could see that they are on their own soul journey. They have been brought into your life as spiritual teachers and supporters. Troubles in adulthood resulting from painful childhoods would shift because you wouldn't stay in the victim game. You know you were in that family to experience what you needed to find or to create more love and forgiveness. See how different your human conditions would feel? Think of how you could create even greater energy for more conscious living using this framework—Spirit first, all else flows.

So let's take as a fundamental premise that your connection to Source comes first. How then do you move to meet your other needs, the ones of the material plane? As you channel and experience higher vibrational energy you radiate out love and peace. You know you are a radiant being of Light and freely share your gifts with others. Your thoughts and beliefs of abundance, love and gratitude draw to you those people and resources you need. You pay more attention to fulfilling your soul contracts than material validation of success. As you become less attached to material things to define you, you allow physical resources to come and go without worry. As you experience set-backs and challenges, you reframe them as opportunities for growth and soul progression.

Instead of interpreting life experiences and conditions as demonstration of being bad or unworthy, you understand what happens is part of your soul journey. You feel better about life and not feel so insecure, unworthy, or disempowered. Like a fresh current of wind, you then feel more energy as you heal wounds of low self worth and self esteem. With greater inner healing you move out into the world energized, feeling renewed and confident.

As you vibrate at a higher energy level you start to draw to you people and resources that match your vibrations and intentions. You affirm that you have all the love and nurturing that you need, and that there is an infinite supply of it. From that place of greater love, you are more willing to share your gifts and resources with others rather than feel a need to horde resources or use force to get what you want. Joy and beauty sweep through your life. Sharing your gifts and resources means you encounter more people who match your energy and you are able to more deliberately manifest for the right highest good of all concerned.

See how this works? Your conscious evolution occurs by tending to your soul awareness and Source Consciousness first and foremost. As you more powerfully channel Source Energy and stand present fully to Love, you meet your needs, not the other way around. As more people awaken, more people understand this process for co-creation and collaborate to achieve success for all.

> *Your conscious evolution occurs by tending to your soul awareness*

There's a marvelous video on YouTube of Patrick Henry Hughes who was born blind, stubs for arms, and deformed back. His parents were devastated at first knowing their child would not be able to run, play, or read like other kids. When he showed a remarkable talent for the piano at the age of 2, his parents knew he was born with other gifts. They held a different intention for their son. As they supported Patrick's gifts for music and the piano, he blossomed. Patrick says in the YouTube interview, at age 20, "God made me blind and unable to walk. *Big deal.* He gave me the musical gifts I have and the great opportunity to meet new people." What a wonderful demonstration of someone living with Yaweh as his foundation and taking life on life's terms, living without sight or legs.

You live with joy and confidence, knowing that Universal Flow is with you continually, appearing in both "good" and "bad" events. This leads you to have much greater energy and freedom to experience the material world as it is. You find ways to be more joyful in your jobs and with your friends, family, and lovers.

When you remember you are Divine Essence, you're able to complete daily tasks more easefully. As you live more in alignment with your soul journey, your relationships with other people blossom and your life tasks get accomplished. You can choose jobs that are more meaningful and help your body stay in better physical health. As you feel good about your mental, emotional and physical health, you feel strong enough to meet the challenges that arise in your life.

Do you get the picture? Your physical world is an outgrowth of your inner spiritual world. Remember—Because Source is limitless, as you connect with that energy, you are a limitless being. It's not that you have to have the right home, the right relationship, the right clothes to live a healthy and happy life. The more you connect with Source, the greater you experience happiness and wholeness, regardless of your specific life conditions at any moment in time.

It is important to release any ideas that you are unworthy, unlovable, and undeserving of Allah's abundance. To become a conscious co-creator you need to give up old notions that you are a sinner, and that God is punishing you for how you life your

> *You alone choose poverty consciousness vs. prosperity consciousness.*

life. Thoughts, attitudes and feelings of poverty, greed, anger, and hatred all block the flow of Source Energy. You alone choose poverty consciousness vs. prosperity consciousness. Regardless of what material resources you have, you can feel rich or poor. Conscious evolution involves tapping into your Divine Essence, remembering Who You Are as a spiritual being.

> Let me stop here and make a *really* important point. Lest we repeat the damaging lessons of the last several hundred years—DO NOT deduce that those who are living with abundance must be specially graced by God and those who struggle now are not receiving God's grace. The material wealth or health of someone *is not* a sign of "salvation" or being "chosen." This line of thinking has lead to centuries of oppression and punitive actions. *We are all capable of receiving abundance. We are all blessed expressions of Divine Essence.*

The paradigm shift that is needed for conscious evolution collectively involves moving past the belief that changes in the physical world are affected only by changes in the physical realm. Cause and effect happen at an energetic level not just at a physical level. Time and Space don't exist in the spiritual realm.

Thus the answers to our complex social issues need to be addressed using a different lens, connected more to Universal Consciousness.

Significant changes in society and in our individual lives can happen instantaneously as we learn to work with our world on an energetic level. The more aware we are of our energy and the more we connect with Source Energy, the faster and more profound the shifts will happen in our lives. Yogis, shamans and mystics have been practicing this Consciousness for centuries. With greater awakening of souls around the planet, these principles are more easily understood and accepted.

The base of the pyramid of the foundation for life, therefore, is to consistently and consciously make decisions and take actions based on your best connection with Consciousness <u>in that moment</u>. As you progress more in your ability to remove your blocks and barriers to the Source of your being, you will be able to stay connected to Consciousness in whatever situation you are in.

This is not to say you won't experience struggles or challenges in your life! I want to make that perfectly clear. You may very well lose your job, have health challenges, end a relationship, etc. These all may need to happen for you to surrender your ego, attachments, or judgments of what 'should' happen so that you may reach out more to your Higher Power, work more intentionally with your Spirit guides, walk more humbly, live more compassionately, and create peace. You may curse your misfortune and wish that things had turned out differently. However, as you constantly come back to the truth of your Divine Essence, you learn to embrace your life events as they unfold. Remember that Universal Energy flows in our lives <u>at all times</u>, whether we see it or not, and whether we understand it or not in that moment.

The key to moving forward is to step out of victim consciousness, release your attachments to outcomes, and shift out of judgments of right/wrong. Avoid asking, "Why did this happen to me?" Don't move back into "poor pity me" or "they are at fault" thinking. This "Stinking Thinking" will drag you down into fear or anger and thus lower your vibrational frequency— and you'll likely take it out on others. That then diminishes others' energy and the conditions around you spiral downward. When you affirm and know that you are experiencing exactly what you need in the moment to help yourself or another shift on their soul progression, you keep your energy vibration higher. Stay focused on love, forgiveness, or compassion to raise your energy level. Esther and Jerry Hicks describe raising your vibrational frequency in their book, *The Amazing Power of Deliberate Intent*, if you want to read more about it.

When you act from the base of Consciousness first, you gain power and strength to do what is yours to do. Rather than clinging to have things turn out a certain way, affirm that the right highest good is done for all involved. You don't have to waste so much energy wishing things were different. You won't stay stuck in struggle. Instead, shift your focus to re-connect with Source in the midst of a challenging situation. Our job is to remember to stay open to channel Source and draw it down to our vibrational frequency so we can share it with the world.

> *When you act from the base of Consciousness first, you gain power and strength to do what is yours to do.*

As you consciously evolve into a 4th dimensional being, hold on to your seat because your life will start to take off in ways you could have never imagined!

Let me end with one final story from Edwina Gaines, a prosperity minister from Alabama. She was traveling in South America with a shaman. They were walking through the jungle and having a difficult time with the heat and physical exhaustion from the trip. Her group kept stopping to rest and drinking energy drinks to keep up their stamina. At one point the shaman laughed and said, "You gringos are so funny. You think you need to get your energy from your food or drinks. All you have to do is this" and he raised his hands looking upward with a loving and joyful heart and asked "Energy please." He made his point fairly clear. The Universal Energy Flow abounds.

End of Chapter Exercises

1. Hold in your consciousness an image of a situation you would like to change or to experience differently. Imagine the situation being resolved and all parties feeling a sense of love, support, and compassion. Practice holding this image 10-15 minutes each day for a month. Note what thoughts come up for you as you hold this image in your awareness.

   a. Do you notice thoughts that negate the loving resolution?

   b. Are your thoughts of receiving and sharing love or are they thoughts of fear, doubts and worry?

   Notice as well what coincidences or subtle shifts happen around you during the time that you do this.

2. Every night for a week bring to mind someone who is physically sick or really struggling with their life conditions. Imagine them being completely free of their struggles and perfectly whole and healthy. Send healing thoughts and intentions to them regularly. If you feel comfortable, ask them how they are open and ready to receive support.

3. Note times when you felt disconnected from your center and inner knowing. Breathe deeply in those moments and imagine a bright light filling your body and emanating out all around you. Raise your vibrational energy by holding an image of yourself perfectly serene, cared for, and secure. Feel the peace and comfort of those thoughts. Breathe that peace in and through every cell, tissue, and organ in your body.

4. Affirm that you have all that you need for your soul contracts and agreements. Feel the energy of these affirmations *as they are currently* true in your life (even if you can't see it in the moment). Hold your awareness on these ideas and feel how it feels to have these true for

your life. Breathe into the peace of each affirmation before reading the next one:

a. All is well in my world and I am secure

b. I feel complete and at peace with all that is in my life

c. I am whole, loved and protected

d. All that I need to fulfill my soul contracts is flowing into my life now and in the future

Part II—Practical Application

CHAPTER 6

❦

Spiritually Aligned Relationships

There's a strange frenzy in my head, of birds flying,
each particle circulating on its own.
Is the one I love everywhere?

Jalaluddin Rumi

The poet Rumi has captured the attention of many readers by his ability to describe eloquently the essence of the ecstatic Divine. He writes of a love that is so human yet carries us to places beyond the human realm. His descriptions of transcendent love sparked by his experience with the mystic Shamz of Tabriz are written in love sonnets of a far different order. The poems have meaning beyond what most Westerners grasp because our notions of love are usually based on romantic or erotic ideas of love. The transcendence that Rumi describes merges the powerful force of the Divine with daily life experiences.

Mystical traditions throughout time have described spiritual transcendence with romantic references. Many have written of God as the Beloved. Wonderful poems and literature over the centuries describe the love affair that comes from being connected strongly with the Holy One. What you feel when you embrace the love and power of the Spirit is quite electrifying. As such it helps to know how to use it well and how to interpret this powerful energy when it flows.

Discerning Three Forms of Love Energy

Experiencing various forms of love energy can be confusing. Sexual or romantic energy and spiritual energy are often intertwined. Spirituality taps into a vast, deep well of that highest, purest form of Love that many crave. Likewise, sexual or romantic relationships carry energy that's easily felt. Just about anyone can feel the electrical charge in the room when two people are passionately embracing or looking at each other in a lustful way.

So how do you discern the spiritual form of love from the romantic form? In the newer stages of a relationship, it is hard to distinguish. Many couples report that when they first met it was like fate brought them together or their union was a gift from God. So, spiritual love and romantic love can feel very similar. Problems can arise when you misread the spiritual form of love as the sexual or romantic form of love.

You who are spiritual seekers or have been awakened to your soul journey likely feel deep emotional intimacy with many people in your life. You probably feel much stronger connections to others who are on the spiritual path. When we connect with those people with whom we feel greater emotional intimacy or spiritual connection it is easy to feel an attraction to them. There almost certainly will be a surge of energy felt, a joyousness. Often you'll feel a "high" from hearing a great spiritual teacher.

It helps to understand what that energy surge is because it is too easy to misattribute those feelings. How can you allow the other person to demonstrate certain qualities ***without*** becoming romantically attached to the other person? The key is to see clearly where the connection and energy come from and how to best react to it.

An elevated energy surge with others can take three forms:

- Spiritual Love energy
- Sexual or Romantic Love energy
- Dramatic Love energy

Spiritual Love Energy:

If you've ever attended a powerful spiritual retreat or event, you know that high amounts of Love energy are generated. The momentary high of the retreat can carry you pretty far. Be very careful about getting too attached to someone you meet at one of these events. The connection you make to someone likely will be charged with the energy from the occasion. That's not to say the person you meet isn't a really wonderful person and worth getting to know. Just be careful about jumping to a conclusion about someone too soon.

When you are in the presence of someone who is really connected to Source or exudes great love and compassion, it is easy to feel attracted to them. Be clear on what that attraction is. It likely is an attraction to their spiritual energy. This energy comes as Spirit, a higher energy than the person per se. "Well, how can that be?" you may ask, "Isn't the person the one who is exuding the energy?" Yes, but the Source of the energy isn't the person, the person serves as the channel through which the energy flows. As Thich Nhat Hanh says, "If someone gives you a glass of water when you are very thirsty, do you give thanks to the person with the glass or the source of the water itself?" You likely will give thanks to the instrument carrying that water, but ultimately your thirst was quenched by the water itself.

You may have felt this kind of Love Energy when singing a favorite hymn or gospel song, or sitting in prayer meetings where the group generates a lot of energy. Feelings of love often arise in spiritual situations. Some call it being zapped by the Holy Spirit. This energy is part of the context of the moment, and is not based simply on the people around you. As the saying goes, 'Whenever two or more of you are gathered, God is there.' Don't get confused between the vessel and the Source.

Attractions or crushes on people who are spiritually-charged are fairly common. You likely will feel good around them, or even feel in love with them. Being present to Love is confusing when you understand it only from a human perspective and not a soul-level perspective. The love you feel in these situations is from a different source than romantic love. This spiritual Love moves through us freely and is shared easily with others. The key is to know when and how to experience this Love devotionally without physical intimacy.

If you find yourself being attracted to someone ask yourself:

> • *What am I attracted to in this person?*
> • *What spiritual experience might I need to have with this person?*
> • *How is this person mirroring some aspect of me that I need to value more?*

These questions can help you gain clarity on what the relationship or encounter means. Perhaps the attraction is occurring to help you move through a particular challenging time in your life. Maybe the other person is there to help you heal from a past scar. Maybe you are there to experience new ways to show and receive love. Physical intimacy may allow you to access this higher spiritual energy, though it is not necessary to achieve a state of connection with the Divine.

> *In the early morning hour, just before dawn, lover and Beloved wake and take a drink of water. She asks, "Do you love me or yourself more? Really, tell the absolute truth."*
>
> *He says, "There is nothing left of me. I'm like a ruby held up to the sunrise. Is it still a stone, or a world made of redness?"*
>
> *This is how Hallaj said, "I am God" and told the truth!*
>
> *The ruby and the sunrise are one. Be courageous and discipline yourself. Completely become hearing and ear and wear this sun-ruby as an earring.*
>
> Rumi

Romantic love energy:

Attraction comes in different ways and can be understood on many levels. Often when you are attracted to someone you are brought together to experience something. God's classroom is relationships. You learn unique lessons in romantic relationships.

If past relationships have tripped you up, look for ways to get closer without being romantically or physically involved with another too soon. That can be a real challenge, especially when your hormones are speaking louder than caution. If you meet someone who is emotionally, intellectually, physically and spiritually appealing, sparks fly.

Those who have trouble with boundaries, perhaps because of inexperience with healthy boundaries, need to practice handling such attractions. Take the opportunity to develop respect or demonstrate support for yourself and your partner.

Time allows the relationship to unfold the soul lessons involved. Time apart from your love interest provides the opportunity to find out why he or she is in your life at this time. Relationships always provide opportunities for growth, healing, loving, and renewing. Honor and celebrate what you have to share with your partner while also being aware of your motives, boundaries, and woundedness that may be triggered with this person.

One fallacy of marriage is that you will never be attracted to anyone else again. As you grow on your spiritual journey, you will come into contact with many beautiful people, on the inside and out. You'll share greater emotional intimacy as well. It gets tricky when you don't know what to do with that attraction. That energy surge can be quite powerful. If one of you is already committed to another person and doesn't know how to handle the energy, it can get messy.

If there are other compelling reasons for you not getting involved, such as you just got over a heart break and need some time to heal, or you are co-workers and it would be disruptive to the work place, then you may need stronger boundaries. Allow more time and space for the attraction to unfold as it needs to. You may need to physically distance yourself by not spending time alone together.

Intimacy can be confusing at times. Recognize emotional intimacy as distinct from physical intimacy. When we spend time getting to know someone on a deeper level or find out things about them that others don't know, the attraction or tension gets intensified. Sharing the stories of your life with one another and knowing each other's pain and joy can be quite fulfilling. There is great attraction in finding those deeper ways to know another. This kind of intimacy, or 'Into-Me-See', often builds strong bonds between people. It is like sharing a secret that no one else knows.

Taking things slowly may be tough when your well is dry and you want to fill it up quickly with this other person's energy. That's why rebound relationships can be so intense, and you may very well need to go through that intensity. However, if your vessel has cracks, your partner could pour all their love into you and you still wouldn't be filled up. Pay attention to how you are receiving and giving your energy with another in these cases. Being clear on your motives and intentions with the relationship, physically or emotionally. This can save you some heart ache further down the road.

Check your mental and emotional state during the heady and heart pounding initial stages of a romantic relationship. If you are going through a rough time at work or dealing with difficult health or family issues, this person may seem like a remedy for your pain. Sometimes you'll just go with the energy flow and see what happens. As a minister friend counseled me many years ago, "move forward, just keep your eyes open." And perhaps falling for someone is exactly the experience you need to go through to learn something about yourself or do the healing work you need to do. Falling and bouncing back is all part of the game.

Be alert to your partner's emotional state. Is it balanced and clear or is it unbalanced and confused? Perhaps you or your partner need to be comforted, either by physical contact or doing fun things to escape some emotional pain. Know that the role you play with each other during this time may be temporary, thus the relationship may be bound by those circumstances. As soon as those circumstances shift or you feel roles changing in the relationship, you may hit some bumpy times. These shifts could be temporary or permanent.

We construct emotional boundaries, consciously or not. Those boundaries determine where your emotional energy goes and what energy you want to receive. Those of you familiar with this know how to channel your energy towards or away from someone as needed. For those of you less familiar with directing your energy, let me give you an example.

> *We construct emotional boundaries, consciously or not.*

If you've ever been with someone you don't like, you probably can easily set your boundaries and not to get too close to that person. You probably won't spend a lot of time talking to them. You don't stand near where they are standing, you don't make as much eye contact, you feel more guarded or emotionally shut down with them. You do certain things that indicate you are not interested in having a conversation or making too much of a connection.

The reverse is also true. If you really like someone you may make greater eye contact or hold the eye contact longer. You may try to stand closer, if not even flirtatiously touch them. You may laugh at their jokes, offer flattery, or in other ways indicate that you are pleased with the other person. You may try to show off your talents more or do something to make a bigger impression. It's all part of the attraction and dating game when we are "on the market" for a new relationship.

Romantic relationships or sexual flirtations can be enormously fun. They get in the way when we mistake someone's spiritual energy for a romantic attraction or when people use romantic energy solely to fill their own needs and don't respect other people's boundaries.

Dramatic love energy:

You probably know people who like creating relationship drama. They like holding their partner in suspense as a form of power trip or thrill seeking. Others like to get caught up in the lives of people by telling the latest gossip of who was with whom. For the spiritually awakened person, those dramas get old—really fast. Getting caught in the latest tidal waves of emotions can be draining and too turbulent. If you have a friend who seems to keep creating such dramatic relationships, you may have to put boundaries on how often you hear their sob story. If you want to keep your balance, try to avoid these continual love dramas, directly or indirectly. That's shifting sand that you don't need to stay in.

If you are creating or experiencing continual drama in your love life, pay attention to the patterns. You may be allowing someone to be close to you because it helps you feel strong, important, or even superior. That's a big trap. Not only is that very ego-based, it's also very fleeting. Because the moment that person challenges you or they don't agree with what you want, you'll feel threatened or lose your attraction. One or both of you may experience pain when motives are unexpressed.

You may be allowing someone to be close to you to keep them dependent on you or for you to stay dependent on them. If you choose to remain dependent on them, you are not finding your own strength. If you help your partner stay dependent on you, you deny him the opportunity to find his own strength. Maintaining or creating dependencies almost always sets up imbalanced and unstable relationships.

For those of you who have had boundaries violated in the past, you may need to practice keeping a greater distance from people for a time. You may see that you don't need to have a certain type of person in your life to make your life complete or validate your sense of self. Look at how you allow others to enter into your personal space, not just physically but emotionally as well.

- *Do you continually agree to do things with someone because you feel guilty saying no? Do you feel uncomfortable honoring your own needs?*
- *Do you let someone stand physically close to you because you think it might be rude to step away?*
- *Are you letting someone else define who you are without looking inward to determine who you are as a spiritual being?*

Consider these questions regarding those who are close to you at this point in your life:

> • *Why have I drawn them into my life?*
> • *What lessons do we need to learn together?*
> • *What experiences are we having that are similar to other relationships in my past?*

Some people like to create continual emotional dramas because it makes life seem interesting or challenging. Entering into or breaking up relationships create emotional and highly charged energetic times. Hitting the highs and lows may be a form of thrill seeking for some people. If you don't want this kind of turbulence, see if there is a pattern to your relationships. Note the red flags.

> • *Do you feel your energy getting jerked around by this person? Does she have a history of crash and burn relationships?*
> • *Is he going through a turbulent episode in life (job or recent relationship transition)? If so, he may be creating this attraction to get sympathy or support but not really interested in a relationship.*
> • *Does she use drugs or alcohol or seem to like high risks or extreme challenges? If so, she may just be using this as another thrill seeking "high" experience.*

You or your partner may be a prime candidate for love dramas if you answer yes to any of these questions. That's not to say that you shouldn't take the risk and move forward with this person. Just know that you may be setting yourself up for another drama.

A note about Friendships:

Friendships are another aspect of important relationships in our life. Platonic relationships, Agape love, or brotherly/sisterly love that is felt between friends can be quite deep and is to be honored and cherished.

We usually feel happy and content with close friends, especially those with whom we talk about more intimate aspects of our life. Generally friendships don't have the same kind of energy surge that we feel when we are sexually attracted to someone. Friendships tend to be more clear-cut. We know when a close friendship is developing. Except for friendships that could turn into romantic relationships, people don't usually get confused about the energy with their friends.

Even if we have an argument or falling out with a friend, generally this energy shift isn't as confusing as the energy that comes from romantic, spiritual, or dramatic love. If you get into a cycle of on-again, off-again friendship, then the friendship probably slips into the category of dramatic relationships. So while we may shift our feelings with friends, or have periods of closeness and absences, friendships tend to be stable relationships that help ground us in our daily life.

Friendships also can unfold on a metaphysical level. You may have experienced meeting someone for the first time and have a sense of familiarity with them. Some friendships click right from the beginning, like you've known each other for years. Consider this—perhaps you have, but not in this life time. It may be that you were part of a family, tribe, clan or friends in a previous lifetime. Michael Newton, in his book *Life Between Lives*, describes soul groups. This is a concept that helps explain those kinds of friends that seem to begin right away, as though you are picking up where you left off. Soul groups may be from any time period, location, or multiple incarnations. An experienced hypnotherapist or past-life regression facilitator can help you re-connect with members of your soul group to better understand a pattern with someone this life time or explain a soul contract that you need to fulfill.

Energy Fields of Your Body

Much has been written about energy fields around our physical body; this is not New Age thinking. Ancient esoteric traditions considered these energy fields to be various levels of consciousness that may be altered with spiritual practices such as yoga or deep meditation.

According to different esoteric and mystical traditions, our physical body is the primary vehicle we use on the earth plane. Many levels of energy fields surround our physical body. They have been grouped together and called by different terms depending on the tradition (such as auras, subtle bodies, biofield, and koshas). People who are able to see auras are able to detect the energy fields surrounding the body. If there is an imbalance or hole in these fields, the physical body will experience illness or discomfort of some sort—physically, mentally or emotionally. Various body work, or in some cases spirit releases or soul retrieval, may be necessary to restore a person to balance. Shamans throughout history in various cultures have done this sort of healing.

According to esoteric philosophies, there are four to nine different energy fields surrounding your physical body that impact us though, not consciously. These include the astral, celestial and other spiritual dimensions. The higher frequency energy fields connect us to one another at the transpersonal or collective soul level. The energy fields closest to your body, which directly affect your physical body, are called the etheric field, or subtle body energy fields.

Barbara Brennan's work outlines three primary ways that people give and receive energy. Her work describes how couples interact energetically as well as group energy. According to Brennan, we generally either take energy from another, get sucked into giving them our energy, or we give and take freely with another without coercion or force. Generally when we have wounds related to loving others we use either of the first two ways of getting energy from others.

According to the ancient Hindu texts of the Upanishads, sexual union constitutes a fire sacrifice bringing together the energy of the partners. Kundalini is sexual energy in its raw form, and through meditation and breathing techniques it converts into higher spiritual energy (energy vibrating at extremely high frequencies). In order to reach this higher state of spirituality, each partner must open up their body through meditation and breath control so that Kundalini energy can be released in the right time and manner. In tantric practice, you can achieve spiritual union or moment of enlightenment at the climax of sexual union.

Kundalini is considered very powerful sexual and spiritual energy. Kundalini means "coiling" and is often depicted as a snake spiraling up one's spine. It is metaphoric for the spiraling consciousness and raised energy that occurs as we achieve greater levels of enlightenment and clearer thought. Kundalini energy comes forth as powerful sexual energy and is considered the female energy in all of us. The awakening of this energy and the manifestations of its power reveal our potential for creativity and union with the Divine Source. Kundalini energy also can be felt as a powerful life force that pulses through us during times of intense devotion or ecstatic spiritual practice.

When you feel Kundalini surge through you it often feels like intense arousal. Indeed, most people who write about Kundalini caution people against trying to open up too quickly to this energy because your physical body could not handle such extreme energy. Kundalini energy is considered so intense that if one hasn't prepared for it through study and practice, the result of unleashed Kundalini would be extreme, resulting in physical or emotional illness, even madness.

Chakras are another way that you can think of energy moving through and around your bodies. Chakras are energy centers that correspond to different areas of your body. In the Hindu tradition the chakras are considered psychic centers that correspond to different levels of consciousness. They are thought to be situated in the etheric or subtle body, not the physical body. More western interpretations of the chakras situate them along the spine starting in the sacrum and rising up to the head.

Regardless of the tradition to explain the chakras, all traditions indicate that each chakra corresponds to a different aspect of your life. The common understanding is that there are seven major chakras and each chakra has a different energy and serves a different purpose in your life. It is believed that the upper chakras higher in the body refer to higher levels of spiritual consciousness.

Integrating your physical body with higher level spiritual energy involves clearing and opening all seven chakras so that energy can flow through you more easily. Understanding the chakra system may give some insights to successes or challenges you have in relationships and other areas of your life. If a chakra is blocked or too open, you will experience an illness or emotional difficulty in the domain of that chakra. Acupuncture, yoga, cranial sacral therapy, Reiki, and other forms of healing are good options for clearing blocks in certain chakras and allowing your energy to flow more evenly.

> *If a chakra is blocked or too open, you will experience an illness or emotional difficulty in the domain of that chakra.*

If you are interested to learn more details, there are many books on chakras. I merely want to introduce the chakras and how they work in your life and relationships. This framework will help you see the connection between your physical body as a vessel for channeling spiritual energy with or without your partner and for health and vitality on many levels.

The first chakra is referred to as the Root chakra ("Muladhara" in Sanskrit) and corresponds to the base of the spine. It has to do with our survival instincts and feelings of being safe and grounded on the physical plane. If this chakra is blocked, you likely will feel continually insecure about basic survival needs, such as food or shelter or safety. This chakra serves your sense of self preservation.

The second chakra, often referred to as the Spleen or Sacrum chakra ("Svadhisthana" in Sanskrit), corresponds to the lower abdomen and genital area. It is important to sexual energy and creativity. Many people who have imbalance here will be either too sexual or shut down sexually with others. This chakra may also correspond to wild ecstatic states of energy that can result in bursts of extreme creativity. This center serves your sense of self-gratification.

The third chakra ("Manipura") corresponds to the Solar Plexus or gut area. The solar plexus is where many consider our life force energy to be centered (in martial arts referred as Hara energy). If this area is blocked you may experience various organ illnesses or a wide range of emotional instabilities. This chakra serves your sense of ego, will, or power.

The fourth chakra, known as the Heart chakra ("Anahata"), corresponds to our heart and lungs, and extends out the arms and hands. It is associated with issues related to relationships and deeper loving (of parents, children or ourselves). If this chakra is blocked, you may feel shut off from others emotionally or unable to open up in loving ways. When this chakra is open and the energy is flowing well, you will experience the integration of love and deep peace. This center serves your sense of self acceptance and compassion.

The fifth chakra, the throat chakra ("Vishuddha"), corresponds to the ability to communicate thoughts and feelings effectively. It is associated with being able to speak your truth, to feel you are heard by others, and to not be silenced. If this area is blocked you will feel you cannot express yourself safely or that others will not listen to what you have to say. This center serves in self expression and creativity through language or sound vibrations.

The sixth chakra corresponds to the mid-forehead, referred to as the Third Eye chakra ("Ajna"). This chakra is associated with light, seeing life clearly, and using intuition effectively. If this chakra is blocked you fail to see things as they are or not see the bigger picture of life. When open, this chakra allows you to experience higher levels of spiritual consciousness. This chakra serves the ability for self reflection and deeper wisdom.

The seventh chakra, corresponding to the top of the head, is known as the Crown chakra ("Sahasrara"). This is considered the channel to Spirit. If this chakra is open you can draw down fully the energy from Source. It is your connection that allows you to receive messages from spiritual guides or connect to etheric images. If this chakra is blocked you will feel disconnected from your Divine Essence and may not trust spiritual messages. This chakra helps you achieve transcendent knowledge, understanding and connection to the Oneness.

In summary, the chakras correspond to places in your body where energy can flow easily or be blocked. Each chakra represents different qualities that are needed to build a whole and integrated life. No chakra is more or less important than another. They all form a unified system of energy that flows through you. When fully open and integrated, you achieve wholeness and balance.

Chakra Alignment with your Partner

It is important not only to clear your own chakras and open the flow of energy in your body, but you can see your relationship as the "body" where the chakras allow energy to flow freely or are blocked. Looking at a relationship as the collective body you can find the best ways to keep energy flowing through your relationships.

The Root chakra represents security and connection to the physical world. So too in relationships we need stability and security in order to feel safe enough to be vulnerable and open. Those people who have not worked through their personal security issues often will be drawn to others who challenge or help them feel secure. If someone continually feels insecure about life, they carry that insecurity in the relationship. Problems will occur around trust and security at some point.

When you feel safe within yourself you will be able to move through the vulnerable times with your partner effectively. When you feel scared or unsafe in the relationship, examine what's triggering your insecurities. Deal with the source of that fear directly. It may be an old fear that your partner is triggering. Doing body work to clear and balance your energy will help shift your relationship. When your root chakra energy flows easily, you will have more stability to deal with the stressors that occur with your partner.

The second chakra relates to the sexual or creative energy in your life. A healthy and vibrant sex life helps a relationship keep energized. Relationships can get stuck or torn apart because this aspect is blocked or shut down. If you feel stuck in a rut in your relationship, you may have a block in your second chakra. Look for more ways to be creative with each other. Are there things you need to birth or create together? It may be that your sexual energy isn't flowing well. Be honest and intentional with your partner about what is working well in this area and what you each need in order to be more open.

One or both of you may be blocked because of your issues related to sexuality. To clear a block in this area, you each need to be comfortable with the role that sex plays in your life. Often sex represents power, control, pleasing or submission. Sex with a partner allows for all of these aspects of your life to emerge. How are you each trying to get what you want from the other sexually? Are you offering yourself from a place of comfort and love or from a place of ego or woundedness? If you have been taught that sex is used for power or that sex is something to be ashamed of, you likely have a block in your second chakra. This block will manifest some way in your relationship, perhaps in your ability to be sexual, intimate, creative or expressive.

You will be able to be more open and expressive with your partner as you work through any past negative experiences or beliefs related to your body or sexuality. A clear second chakra means you are more receptive to your partner and you won't spend energy covering up a wound that may be blocking the energy flow. Sex can become playful and joyful rather than distressing or painful.

According to Tantric traditions, sexuality and spirituality are intertwined. Kundalini energy is described as a serpent that climbs up our spine along each chakra connecting Shakti (the female energy) with Shiva (the male energy). Temples in old town Katmandu show graphic depictions of sexual union. They display the belief that the Divine is expressed and experienced at the moment of orgasm. For most Westerners this is shocking because we aren't used to seeing sex and spirituality mixed and being represented in a holy place such as a temple. Yet sexual union can be a holy and sacred act, tapping into a powerful energy force of Spiritual Source. Lovers who have cleared their second chakra can connect to the power and radiant love of the Divine Essence during sex.

In the Tantric tradition sex is worshipful experience of the Divine Essence. Tantric sex is considered a ritualized form of worship such that being orgasmic is a physical prelude to a greater spiritual energetic state. Reaching an orgasmic state as a spiritual practice (either alone or with a partner) is considered a mindful path of spiritual ecstasy. Teachers of the Tantric tradition would have males practice delaying ejaculation while in a state of sexual arousal to build up Kundalini energy, while encouraging women to let it flow more freely. Chants, meditations and breath control are other ways to strengthen holding Kundalini energy when in a state of arousal until the time is optimal to express the union with the Divine.

The third chakra, the solar plexus, represents your will or personal power. If your relationship is stagnating it may be that this chakra is stuck or blocked. What do you each need to do to bring your own will into greater alignment with a Higher Power? See if you are giving over your power to your partner or if you are taking power away from your partner for your own safety or ego. Are you playing the victim and giving up your power so you won't need to be responsible for how you are living your life? Don't give up your power or refuse to take responsibility for who you want to be and what kind of life you want to live. On the flip side, examine whether you are dominating or manipulating your partner to get your way.

How are you feeding energy into the relationship and what type of energy are you sending? Are you operating from a victim and scarcity mentality? A dominance and control mentality? Examine carefully what is preventing the energy from flowing from your center of love and compassion. The power chakra is critical. Many relationships die or wither here. Step back enough from your situation to be honest about what game your human small self (ego) is playing. See what adjustments you need to take to open the blocks that are preventing Divine Essence from coming through. Are you willing to let go of whatever is keeping those blocks there? When you are able to let go of whatever is keeping you in the victim or domination mindset, you will be able to create a more loving and healthy relationship. You have to be willing and able to let go of those old patterns that hold you back to open up this chakra. Will and power, surrender and acceptance are balanced in this third chakra.

Sometimes it is scary to move forward into alignment with a greater spiritual presence because your partner may not be able to do it with you. They may stay stuck in their blocks even as you've cleared yours away. This will have to be a decision and trade-off for you to consider. We are at a point in human evolution that contrasting vibrational energy relationships won't last. As you do your clearing and healing work, you will naturally move towards higher vibrational relationships.

> *We are at a point in human evolution that contrasting vibrational energy relationships won't last.*

Be prepared to let go or distance yourself from colleagues, family members, or love relationships that don't resonate with where you are spiritually. They no longer serve you or allow you to stay connected to your Higher Power. And if you stay in the lower vibrational energy relationships, you will not help them either. They must choose a better way for themselves; you cannot do this work for them.

If you have cleared the first three chakras and are primarily living connected to the energy of Divine Essence, you will be operating with greater vibrational energy than the first three chakras. If your partner is struggling with chakra levels 1-3 and you shift to operate beyond the fourth chakra, the relationship in all likelihood will not survive long. A relationship cannot be sustained if both partners are operating more than 2 chakra levels apart (one of you is working through chakra levels 1-3 and the other works with chakra energy 5-7). The dissonance of those very different energy vibrations will be too great to sustain.

Some relationships progress beyond the solar plexus chakra where you both have opened the flow of energy and operate with similar energy levels. Staying connected to your Higher Power on a more regular basis allows you to access energy and insights from chakra levels four through seven. The fourth chakra is the heart chakra. That is a fun place to be with your partner. You are both able to move in loving harmony with each other, offer love easily, and accept your partner for who he or she is, flaws and all. This type of love comes from being open to the love that flows authentically through each of you and has a Source greater than both of you. Spirit shines forth brightly in the heart chakra, and you feel the warmth and love even in the midst of challenging times in your relationship.

An open fifth chakra, the throat chakra, means you each speak your truth honestly and compassionately with one another. You don't sit in judgment of one another but share your viewpoints and opinions with openness and compassion. You know you each have your own filters through which you see the world, and you share your ideas and views with that greater understanding. With a clear fifth chakra you can hear each other more honestly and ask for what you need. You can state your views without fear of rejection or ridicule, and you can ask questions of your partner without blaming, criticizing or condemning. You aren't trying to change your partner's worldview or force your ideas on to them. You simply offer what is your truth and let that truth be spoken without attachments to what the other will do with it. Connecting to Source, you honor your partner's views and don't cling to your ego's desire to be right.

The sixth chakra corresponds to the "third eye" (middle of forehead) and this is the point through which higher consciousness and clarity flows. If you resonate with your partner at this level you are each able to receive and give this wisdom freely. You share insights and see new lessons as they emerge. You are each a clear mirror for one another and help each other see situations for the spiritual experiences that they are. As you are able to stay connected to your Higher Power most of the time, you can offer understanding and clarity without getting ego-involved in the situation. You have the patience and skill to stay open to seeing things for what they are and to wait for the unfolding to happen in the divine right timing that is needed without forcing your way.

The seventh chakra, the crown chakra, is the portal of Light and Love that can descend through you. A relationship that functions at this level is very rare indeed. The relationship is focused on the highest flow of energy and in alignment with the Source for all your actions. You are able to offer your love for the greatest good of all beings completely detached from the outcomes. You are not operating out of the ego but purely from a place of unconditional love for all. You have nothing at stake and nothing to achieve but simply being a Light for others.

I have met very few couples that function at the level of the seventh chakra. The one or two occasions where I have seen couples functioning at this level, it is a delight to experience. Both people are moving freely in their own Light and offering that Light and Love freely to their partner. That's not to say that they don't have difficulties, challenges or crises. They move through it first and foremost with God Consciousness as their compass. They live genuinely, lovingly, compassionately, intentionally, and openly.

The best way to move through the chakras with your partner is for each of you to pay attention to your own healing and tend to the blocks as they emerge. You each need to be willing to do the work that is needed to clear your own blocks and provide support for each other as you do this work. It requires courage and stamina to get through the clearing process. Couples who can do this individually and together feel much closer and committed.

When you are going through a stressful time, either personally or with your partner, step back and look for what is being shown to you about your soul journey and who you want to be in the relationship. Explore whether your energy is blocked in one of your chakras. A relationship struggle will usually have something to do with your core issues related to that chakra. If you are experiencing stress in your relationship, recognize and honor the opportunity to respond or operate differently. Such tension is a gift for you and your partner. If you see it as a gift and take time to work through what is being triggered, staying connected to Source, you'll find your way through the issue. You and your partner are doing what your souls have agreed to do with each other. This is how you evolve together.

> *You and your partner are doing what your souls have agreed to do with each other.*

If you are struggling in a relationship, recognizing it as part of your soul contract helps ease any pain or judgments about what is happening. You recognize that your challenge is all divinely planned for your soul progression. It is up to each of you to awaken so that you can live your higher purpose with one another. Periods of "Divine Discontent" can be enormously challenging, yet fruitful if you can shift to a stronger connection with one another's Divine Essence. Your relationship can become a playful experience bringing out the best energy of your chakras for the highest good of all.

Remember that you are each responsible for your own growth, joy, and healing. You each must make a choice as to how you want to deal with your life conditions. You don't have to carry the burden of your partner's work and ultimately can't do their work for them. Remembering your relationship as a spiritual unfolding, you can ask for guidance and assistance of your Higher Power and guides to work with you through the situation.

Understand that you each will have blocks in different chakras as your primary work to clear. On any given day you may feel blocked in one or several chakras. Most couples falter because of blocks they experience in the first few chakras. As you clear your chakras and get into greater alignment and balance with your energy, you will feel a greater flow of energy in your relationship and other areas of your life.

As soul-filled partners, dance in the joy of the glorious ways you give and receive love. Let the ecstasy fill you from your toes to the crown of your head and beyond.

End of Chapter Exercises

1. For those people with whom you share intimate moments, determine what you might need to experience with them for joy, love, growth or healing. Review the questions presented in this chapter as it might relate to this person. Pay attention to patterns of how you have related to people intimately.

2. To embrace the fullness of Who You Are and accept the shadow in yourself and others in your life, here's a visualization you can use.

   • Work with a partner for whom your relationship matters and which relationship you want to strengthen.

   • Sit facing your partner and have your partner read the following while you keep your eyes closed.

   Imagine a white or gold light coming over you and bathing you in love, comfort, peace and compassion . . . . Feel the warmth of love, comfort, peace and compassion move through your body, starting with the top of your head and working down through your face . . . neck . . . shoulders . . . moving into your chest and filling your heart and lungs with warmth and compassion. Now send that light down through your torso . . . . into your hips . . . now down your legs and into your feet. See the light now filling your whole body so that you are glowing with love and compassion.

   As you feel compassion moving all through you, summon to your awareness one quality that you don't like to admit you have. Invite this quality to reveal itself and hold it like you would a small child that needs comfort. Greet this quality and speak it aloud.

   "I welcome you _____. I know you are part of who I am." Sit with this quality a while . . . . What is the gift of this quality? How might it serve you at times?

   Embrace this quality as an integral part of who you are . . . .

*Now think of an object that represents this shadow quality . . . .
Imagine giving the object to your partner with thanks that he/she will
accept it and embrace it as a part of you. How does it feel to have your
partner accept this part of you?*

*Affirm that your partner will have compassion and understanding as
you express this quality in your relationship.*

When you feel complete with this visualization, trade places and read
this visualization to your partner. Discuss what comes up for each of
you from this exercise.

3. If you are struggling in your relationship, it's likely that you are playing
    out some sort of dynamic or drama that is unfinished business. This
    could be from a past life time or with someone close from an earlier
    time in your life. Answer these questions:

    *   *What aspects of your partner bother you that are similar to previous
        people in your life with whom you have had troubles?*
    *   *How is your partner helping you open to the beauty of who you are?*
    *   *What soul contracts do you think you are here to fulfill with each
        other?*
    *   *What are the challenges in your relationship saying about who you are
        and who you want to be?*
    *   *Are there shadow elements in your partner that you don't want to
        admit are within you?*

4. Review past relationships or flings/affairs you've had. Is there any
    pattern to the type of person you've drawn into your life regarding
    their emotional or spiritual state? Have you seen times when you've
    drawn people to you when you've been in certain emotional states?

5. If you've felt shut off from others emotionally or physically, what may
    be preventing your heart from opening up to others? Is there some trust
    that's been violated or healing that needs to happen? Working with the
    chakras through meditation or physical work can help you heal those
    wounds. See Suzann Robins' website http://www.suzannrobins.com/
    for more information on this work.

CHAPTER 7

❦

The Power and Meaning of Money

Whatever form we are, able or disable, rich or poor, it's not how much we do, but how much love we put in the doing.

Mother Teresa

One of the biggest areas of shifting sand in daily life has to do with money. The economic meltdown of 2008 brought home the need to get clear on what money actually means. Having a healthy and conscious relationship with money includes knowing what money represents for you. When you can align how you use money with your inner world of values and spirituality, you'll be able to navigate through challenging economic times.

I like to use Jacob Needleman's book, *Money and the Meaning of Life*, for class discussion of business ethics. It is a fabulous book to get people to reflect on the power of money in their life, and more importantly, on the beliefs they have about money and what money represents. According to Needleman, we can never really use money well in our life if we don't understand the meaning we derive from it. For some people money means security. For others it means status, respect, independence etc. Unless we know what money means for us, we'll never have a healthy relationship with it. Money will control you rather than you controlling your money.

In his book Needleman asks readers to determine what use money has for their internal world and external world. Needleman's idea of external and internal world corresponds to my description of the physical world (outer) and the spiritual world (inner). The more you integrate these worlds, the more authentic you'll live and the more intentional you'll be in how you use money. The external world is usually fairly easy for people to address.

You see that you need money for transportation, housing, food and clothing. Those are the external ways you use money for things that support your material comforts and your physical necessities.

What about your inner world, your spiritual life? How are you using money to support that? Are you providing the resources (money and other resources) to support a rich inner life as much as you support your outer world? If not, why not? Do you <u>desire</u> a rich inner world to the same degree you desire a rich outer world? If not, why not?

It's been said if you want to know what's important to someone look at their calendar and their check book. The two commodities seen as most precious today are time and money. How are you using these to reflect Who You Are?

> *How are you using money to support a rich inner life?*

Money is perhaps one of the most powerful tools in our modern era for saying who we are, showing our inner world through our outer world of possessions and lifestyle. Look at your life today and see how money has defined who you are—by where you live, where you have traveled, the recreational activities you do etc. Do you share your money freely with others, strangers or family? Are you afraid of money—how to ask for it, how to use it, how to have it?

The power and meaning you give to your money determines how you live your life. Your ability to integrate a rich spiritual life with material possessions reflects how well you bring your values, beliefs and best intentions into your world. Are you expressing your spiritual world the way you desire in your physical world?

Money itself (whether in paper form or electronic data recorded somewhere) is just that—paper or digits. Money in paper or digital form is exchanged for goods and services or sometimes other pieces of paper. Money is merely a tool for expressing and experiencing life.

I like to share this story to demonstrate that money represents faith more than anything else.

Perhaps this is what the Founding Fathers of America knew when they inscribed on our currency "In God We Trust".

On a trip to Nepal I bought a bus ticket from Katmandu to the Royal Chitwan National Preserve. I somewhat confidently gave my money to the bus operator for a piece of paper that had, from what I could see, just chicken scratches on it. The piece of paper was written in some local script. For all I knew the paper said, "You stupid Westerner, you just gave me money for a worthless piece of paper."

I checked to be sure I had bought the right ticket to leave in the morning to where I wanted to go, "Will I be able to get on this bus in the morning with this ticket to go to Chitwan." The driver responded with a smile, "Allah providing." I knew that was the best I was going to get as confirmation of my ticket.

I've since thought of that driver's response. As surprised and somewhat unsettled as I was when I heard it, I have since realized what a profoundly truthful statement that was. We'll get wherever we're going with the grace of God or 'God willing and the crick don't rise.' We did in fact get to Chitwan, though only after a six hour delay. A bus ahead of us had fallen off the road at a spot where the road had washed away. We spent the time playing cards with other tourists while we waited for a truck to arrive from Katmandu to haul the other bus to the next town. Allah provided a sunny day at least for us to play cards on the mountain side.

The Meaning of Money—What's of Value to You?

It's said that the Mayan and Aztec cultures had no use for the gold that the Spanish explorers offered. They had all that they needed so the gold from the Spanish wasn't valuable to them. It was only when these indigenous people found other things the white Europeans had that were valuable to them that exchanges took place. Money, currency in whatever form, is an exchange of things people value.

> Money, currency in whatever form, is an exchange of things people value.

I had an interesting conversation once with a couple of businessmen. During the course of it one of them said he doesn't mind taking risks, even ones that seem to defy economic sense. He shared a story of how he renovated an office building he owned and in doing so he reduced the number of rental units. He liked what he had designed and commented that what he had done made no economic sense but he was proud of his building. To my ears he was repeating the old tune that completely distorts classical economics. In his mind, and many others, economics is about money and profits.

I stopped him and said that he thought of economics in a bastardized way. Most people equate economics with the study of money. Actually classical economics is the study of **utility** and how people make exchanges in order to maximize utility. Utility is anything that brings pleasure <u>or has value for us</u>. Once we shift from seeing economics as money to seeing economics as utility, we immediately have a new paradigm to work from. We no longer chase money as the goal, but instead focus on utility—that which brings us pleasure or value. One of the silver linings in the cloud of the economic tumble in 2008-2009 is that it forced people to get really clear on what they valued.

For this businessman to have taken out two stories of his building to make room for an atrium and art gallery may have made <u>perfect</u> classic economic sense. If he valued space for plants or artwork as something that brought him or others pleasure, even if it meant he couldn't rent the space to make money from it, it was a <u>rational</u> economic decision. I then gave a five minute oration that too many people have come to equate rational economic decisions with maximizing <u>money</u> rather than maximizing what we <u>value</u>, or utility.

A primary economic premise is that people are "rational" decision-makers. According to classical economics, people make estimates of what their greatest interest is and then base their actions and decisions to maximize that self-interest (preferably *optimize* it in the spirit of "enlightened self-interest"). For example, time with children or purchasing something beautiful is a rational economic decision if that is what you value. Once you see that you are trying to optimize your utility, weighing all those things you do that bring pleasure, beauty, value to your life, you stop focusing on money as the be-all end-all of economic systems. If you focus on those things that bring you value, and in line with your values, then you can make decisions more in alignment with your inner world. This has enormous implications for your personal life as well as our collective life with respect to greed, international trade, taxes and government spending etc.

When I was done with my tutorial, an elderly gentleman who had been sitting near us and listening to my talk came over to us. He said to me, "What you just said in the last five minutes is more insightful than anything I learned in my entire MBA program. It finally made the last 30 years of my career make sense." He shook my hand and then left. And so, one more person was enlightened with a new way of viewing money and economics.

It is precisely because we view money as the driving force in our life that we lose sight of things we value. In so doing we focus on the external world more than our inner world and thus get disconnected from Source. If we turned our thinking around, pay attention to things we value first, and then proceeded to make decisions regarding money to help us obtain those things of value, we'd align our inner world with our outer world. If we value woodlands, how do we make decisions about building and transportation based on maintaining green space? If we value aesthetics, how can we improve our homes and workplaces to bring in more beauty? If we value time with our family, how can we carve out a life to have more of it?

Make decisions about what is important to you first, and then find the resources and tools to bring about those things you value. If you say you value your children or your employees, put forth the time and money needed to ensure healthy children and safe work places with fulfilled workers.

Thus, our examination of the power and meaning of money has to start from the vantage point of what is valued. In order to do this, you need to look at your inner life for that is where you determine what is important to you. The inner world as I'm portraying it involves your values, ethics and beliefs, your authentic self, and your spiritual center.

Money and Power

There is nothing wrong with having or making a lot of money. The questions to consider are how do you use money and what are you willing or <u>not</u> willing to do to obtain money? These are the central questions I pose to my students and workshop participants in my seminar on "Money, Ethics and Values". I like to spend time in these workshops talking about one's inner world, personal journeys, and relationship to money as it reflects people's perceptions of themselves and how they relate to other people. Money is directly tied into your notions of status, power, control, security, beauty, belonging, self-confidence, etc.

My workshop participants are usually astonished when they realize that money plays a <u>huge</u> role in how they relate to other people. Not only does money affect relationships with peers and immediate family, but also it says a lot about your perception of authority (parents, the church, the state, etc.) and power.

Power comes from controlling valuable resources. Again you have to look closely at what is <u>valuable</u> to you. Generally those things that help you meet your needs are valuable. Those needs include love, security, autonomy etc. Money is simply one resource to help meet your needs. Connecting to your Higher Power as your foundation, you'll meet your needs. Creativity, imagination, positive self worth, social and emotional skills all extend from Source as your base. If money is used properly, it can help refine those qualities in you, and help you obtain what you need. Money is simply a tool, not the <u>goal</u> itself. In fact, money can be a contributing factor in <u>not</u> getting your needs met, if used poorly.

Money is a major battleground in relationships. Is money used as power in your relationships? Money often determines who makes the decisions. Financial decisions are frequently a very challenging part of relationships.

Depending on your culture, you may have learned the rule that whoever obtains the most money makes the decisions. One need only look at political financing in the U.S. to see how this is played out.

Money may determine your sense of self. Many people believe that their salary reflects their worth either to the company or society. Income may show how successful a person is in some standardized way, but that isn't a measure of their inherent worth, and rarely an indicator of happiness or spiritual richness. Anyone can take pride in one's work regardless of how much money one makes. If you think your contribution to society is based solely on your income, you miss so many other ways to serve having nothing to do with money.

> - *How do you value yourself?*
> - *How much does your income boost or diminish your sense of self worth?*
> - *Do you allow yourself to be governed by other people's opinion of you as demonstrated by the salary you earn?*

There are certainly plenty of instances of people who make lots of money precisely to boost their sense of self worth. For these people income can be a real trap because their low self-esteem seems to push them to make more money. Like a gerbil in a running wheel, they never feel they have enough. If your feelings of self worth are tied to your money, then you will be like a yoyo, emotionally riding the tides of money as it comes and goes.

"Hold on a minute," you might be thinking. "I need money to provide for my family." There are many ways you can provide for your family—both their inner world and outer world. What are you doing to tend to your own and your family's spiritual and emotional well-being? Do you put as many resources into growing their inner world as you provide for their material world? What other resources besides money can you provide to your family to lead a rich life?

> *What other resources besides money can you provide for your family to lead a rich life?*

Taking time to examine the role that money plays in your sense of self worth, self esteem or self competence can unveil some old beliefs. When you get rocked by fears related to not having enough money, examine where that feeling of lack is coming from. What do you fear is lacking? What kind of security or inner stable ground are you looking for that you think money can provide? Is the lack due to an inner deprivation, a feeling of not being accepted or loved enough by others? If so, how will money or material things change that? Is the lack from your self-limiting beliefs that you aren't good enough, and therefore you don't believe that you deserve more money than what you have? Is the lack due to not trusting Spirit to provide all that you need?

Remember *as you travel your soul journey with an awakened mind, you will find what you need.*

Here is an affirmation to remember you have and <u>are</u> the abundance that you seek:

> *Thank you, Sweet Spirit, for all the abundance in my life. I know I am provided with all I need for the next step in my journey. I take one step at a time, trusting that the next step will be filled with more beauty, wonder, and opportunity for my growth, success, and wholeness. I gratefully and graciously receive all the abundance flowing to me and into my life, from the smallest acts of kindness to the greatest generosity that surrounds me. I welcome and receive all the gifts provided in every kind gesture throughout my day.*
>
> *With this knowing and receiving, I give thanks for being so wonderfully sustained and blessed, and in turn offer my gifts and blessing to those around me for their glorious fulfillment. I affirm that all beings are bountifully blessed, nurtured, and guided to express their Divine Essence and reach their full potential.*

Messages about money shape how we see the world from the time we are young. How generous or stingy we are ties in directly with our views of the scarcity of money, the need to share our blessings, the need to control others, etc. It is worth examining what lessons you learned about love from your family as it related to money.

Was money used as a substitute for love? Did a parent shower you with gifts but not spend time with you or support your activities? Was money used to control others by threats of withholding money if you or others didn't do what a parent or family authority figure said? Was money used to cover up mistakes rather than allowing you to learn from your mistakes?

The American immigrant story and the American dream present the idea that children will have more than their parents had. Yet we forget that the material world is only part of the picture. The yardstick often used in the American success stories is generally money or material things. How can you give your children things you didn't have emotionally or spiritually? What do they need spiritually more than materially?

We see the effects of material wealth without emotional and social wealth in children. All the toys and new technology (cellphones, tablets, and game boxes) don't teach how to get along with others or cope with disappointment or adversity. A rich spiritual life is an invaluable resource in these areas. Too many children are emotionally abandoned, or they have been given stuff to replace the quality time they need with loving, supportive adults. Children experience spiritual impoverishment when they don't receive love, don't see faith in action, or don't develop resiliency to navigate difficult times. In the digital frenzy today with new technology appearing every year, the trap for the latest gadget becomes more gripping. Yet how is that enriching your child's soul?

Money, Justice, and Spirituality

Various faith traditions teach an ethic of caring, hospitality to strangers, of being your brother's keeper. Money often is used to express our beliefs about how much we should take care of others. The phrase Nobles Oblige generally refers to the idea that "For those to whom much is given, much is expected." It came from the idea that the noble class must act responsibility to benefitted those who had less. Though most middle class Americans don't think of themselves as nobility, we still have many opportunities and resources compared to the vast majority of people around the planet. I love to discuss the concept of Nobles Oblige. It stirs many opinions and emotions regarding justice, equality and wealth in a just society.

Most of my students have never heard the phrase Nobles Oblige, yet somehow it permeated their awareness when we talk about topics related to justice and fairness. Is it fair that some few people have a million fold more money than most of the population on the planet? Many people in the US believe that profit or bounty should be distributed based on how hard one worked to earn it. The concept of <u>equity</u>, you get what you earn, is deeply entrenched in the collective consciousness in America.

Few Americans consider the three different rules of fairness: *equity* (you receive in proportion to what you contribute), *equality* (divide the bounty equally regardless of each person's contributions) and *need* (divide the goods according to needs regardless of how much each contributed). Lively discussions can ensue when people discuss which rule of fairness is used (equity vs. equality vs. need) in determining fair distribution of resources—at work, in society, at home. Most people believe that justice is important but few really have delved deeply to wrestle with the complexity of determining fair distribution of resources or wealth. Money is an instrument for creating a just world, or not, depending on which rule of fairness you use.

The 2011 debate by the US Congress to balance the Federal budget had themes of justice. Explicitly they debated—How much money *should* government collect from individuals and corporations and how should it be distributed? I don't believe they fully understood the implicit arguments they were having in their debates—What rules of fairness are we using? What is the social good that we aspire to create with taxes? Justice, spirituality and money intersect at the nexus of financial decisions regarding tax laws, corporate compensation, immigration laws, and health care. These are concrete examples of how our inner world (beliefs about justice) directly impacts our outer world (voting on tax laws or policies on immigration).

The topic that I most like to get people discussing is executive compensation. This became a larger social debate in the aftermath of the banking failure of 2008. Is it fair that an executive who has a lot of responsibility can earn over 1,000 times the amount that the lowest paid worker makes? Many will say yes, executives work hard for their pay and their decisions impacts hundreds if not thousands of others. Thus the responsibility and stress warrants their pay. How can we determine a responsibility-to-pay ratio (or if you want to apply the equity rule, the contribution-to-pay ratio) that makes sense and is just?

I challenge my college students to think about whether they've earned the money they receive from their parents to go to school. Most say they've earned something for working hard in high school to make good grades. Even the students who are paying their own way to school are generally getting some form of government assistance and feel they've earned that assistance.

I also challenge them to explain why they should get money to go to school simply for having done well in high school. I ask them to dig deeper to see if money helped them be successful at school (such as private tutors) or if they had other advantages that other children do not have. Is that fair? Can we create a level playing field for basic things such as education, when children come from families whose parents can't read, aren't home to take care of them, or simply don't care about their education? Clearly the cards are stacked against some kids from very early ages, making it harder to concentrate and do well at school. Considering only equity, the rule of letting people "earn" their way to college, misses the mark if we want to create a world for all to succeed.

Most of my students see their parents as working hard, or they personally have worked to pay their way through school. As such they believe that they or their parents deserve the money they get. Yet they often don't see that their income may come from working for companies that are harming others in another place on the planet. Tying ideas of justice into global capitalism is one point of a business ethics class. The central theme we explore is the Triple Bottom Line of people, planet, profit. The health of people and the planet is inextricably linked to the financial health of a business (profits).

The balanced Triple Bottom Line approach vs. profit maximization articulates what society values. Every society passes laws and provides incentives to support what they value. If a society values the planet and people as much as profits, then taxes and laws to support environmental health and employee health and wellbeing follow. When profit (money) is the primary value, businesses try to minimize (or externalize) their costs to maximize profit. Unless businesses value the planet or people (be it their own employees or the larger community) as much as their profit, their actions are based purely on profit motives. Currently, the link between people, planet and profits is heavily skewed towards profits. If supporting the health of the planet has value to businesses and society, they will find a way to create profits with that goal in mind. Businesses are creative enterprises; they find ways to achieve their goals based on their values.

Even when profit is the primary value, it begs the question—for what purpose is the profit? Business profits support people's wellbeing by providing employee salaries and retirement dividends. What value and meaning do profits (either in income or other forms of wealth) ultimately have for individuals? Is it security, is it prestige, is it recognition of a job well done? I was fascinated when I was in India to learn that the devout Brahman men are expected to give their money away towards the end of their lifetime and offer their life in service. I walked into temples and wondered if the old men sweeping the steps were once business tycoons.

I was told the Hindu Brahman tradition encouraged men to renounce wealth or fame and live simply once they ended their career and took care of family. They give their money away at that time because they recognize they can't take it with them upon death. It also is a humbling approach recognizing that all are here for a finite amount of time. This spiritual tradition encourages business leaders' final contribution to be of service to others, not their own aggrandizement.

How interesting it would be for Donald Trump or Ted Turner to adopt that philosophy. What a different country America would be if billionaires gave away their money to charity and spent their last years doing humble service work. Bill Gates and Warren Buffet are active in recruiting other billionaires to sign a pledge to give away half their wealth before they die.

What do you believe about sharing money with your family versus society as a whole? Estate taxes and financial planning are based on these key concepts of justice whether we articulate them or not. You may recall the story of Jesus turning over the money changer's tables in the temples. The quote of "Render unto Caesar what is Caesar's" is worth examining. What does Caesar represent today? Do you see government playing a role in creating greater social justice? What institutions of power do you want to support with your money? Given the current rules of the game and the entrenched power structures, I don't see a major overhaul of the financial system happening anytime soon.

With the fallout of Wall Street financial institutions and large banks, executive compensation and consolidation of wealth in the hands of a few are social issues of justice gaining more attention. Unless the public is willing to look deeply into their values, rules of fairness, and ethics (inner world) and align them with their voice and their vote (outer world), structural changes in wealth creation or distribution aren't likely to happen. If motivated enough, we can change the flow of money in our society and globally through the various laws regarding corporate governance, wage regulations, environmental laws etc.

What does it mean to "Give unto God what is God's?" Certainly history has shown examples of enormous corruption of church institutions over the centuries. Money has been used for indulgences, salvation, or propping up kings and despots in the name of religion. My interpretation of this phrase is not about supporting a church or religious institution. Instead it's about turning over our thoughts, words and deeds to those aspects that nurture your soul. You'll tend to your soul by giving your time, attention, talent, and money to your highest emotional and spiritual health and sharing that with the world. Money as part of a soul journey entails allocating such resources to help strengthen your inner world. Money, time and other resources support acts of kindness, love and compassion demonstrated in the outer world.

Our spiritual inner world and our material outer world are aligned as we understand the power and meaning of money. Themes of justice abound in many of our daily decisions, personally and collectively. How well we integrate our beliefs of justice and ethic of caring determines the kind of world we create. God/Allah/Great Spirit, most merciful and compassionate, acts <u>through us</u>. As we express our Divine Essence we extend that mercy, graciousness, and compassion. Indeed, as we see God in others, knowing we are all Divine Essence, money is a tool to uplift and embrace the Holy Oneness in all its wondrous forms.

Conscientious Consumerism

Trade has happened for millennia, but the form and speed with which trade happens today is unprecedented. Today's economy is based on abstract numbers being shifted electronically, instantaneously across nations. The mortgage asset swaps across financial and banking institutions is a prime example. We discovered the effects when companies don't look carefully enough at the numbers being shuffled around. Financial managers lost sight of what those numbers represented—people's homes, livelihoods, and families.

One way to change the flow of energy regarding money and power both locally and globally is through purchasing and investing decisions. If we want to change how money flows through our society and around the planet, we need to change how money is spent, either in how we buy from companies or invest in businesses. Every consumer has the power to change the dynamics and flow of money in daily life through their interaction with businesses. How and where people spend their money is under their control.

Where we shop and the types of products we buy impact a long line of people. Every purchase is a result of hundreds if not thousands of people's efforts from design to production to distribution to disposal. John Elkington in his seminal book, *Cannibals with Forks*, proposed a new ideology of consumerism and manufacturing. Part of this shift comes in "waste equals food" planning, such that the by-products of one product can be used as resources for creating another product. Bill McDonough has taken this approach as the basis for his book, *Cradle to Cradle*, in which he reminds us that there is no "away" anymore. We can't keep manufacturing and purchasing throw-away products because there is no such place as "away" on our planet. Thus we need to think "cradle to cradle" rather than use "cradle to grave" throw-away products. People in remote countries who recycle or remanufacture products with toxic chemicals ingest and breathe the waste of the products we use. It requires a shift in thinking from creating throw-away products to constructing products that compost or can be re-used in some fashion for other products.

When you purchase a product, stop and ask yourself these questions:

* *How will the packaging be reused?*
* *How will the product itself be eliminated when you are through with it?*
* *Where will it go and how will it impact the earth when you are done with it?*

Additionally, when you purchase the product, give thanks to all the people whose labor was necessary for you to have this product. Give thanks to Mother Earth and Father Sky for the raw materials that are needed for you to have this product. **Consider what impact you and a product will have on the planet through its use and disposal.** This is a critical first step in conscientious consumerism. Your role as consumer is vital to the health and well-being of people, places and animals everywhere.

Another step is to be intentional with your investments. Look at more than just the percent growth or return on investment. You'll leave your grandchildren more than just money. What kind of <u>world</u> do you want to leave them?

> * *What is your investment creating or supporting?*
> * *What companies are being supported by your investments? Are they creating social good or social ill?*
> * *What kind of social and environmental impact is your investment having, directly or indirectly?*

The web of our existence is woven tightly across the globe; money is a major thread. Your retirement or savings may be growing because of the labor of children in sweat shops or people living in unsanitary conditions. Since the economic downturn of 2008, you may be tempted to do whatever it takes to rebuild your finances. As your investments grow, reflect on what you are willing to accept in exchange for your return on investment. Do your financial investments reflect your values?

> *Do your financial investments reflect your values?*

If you are interested in learning more, research social indices and brokerage firms that specialize in socially responsible investing. Where you shop and invest impacts others even if that impact seems remote. Most people have no idea what companies their retirement funds are supporting. *Take some time in the next month to find out which companies are in your pension portfolio, and see if those companies are helping to create a world you want to live in or not.* Use your money to invest in your values by choosing companies that conduct their business in a socially responsible way, with respect to the environment, worker salaries, human rights, work conditions etc. Through socially responsible investing, you get a two-for-one deal—creating the kind of world you wish to have, and receiving a return on your investment. In other words, you are spiritually enriched financially by having your inner world and your outer world aligned.

How money is used is anything but value-free. The predominant economic system in place (free market capitalism) has inherent values to it. One such value is individual private property. Globally this has significant repercussions. A simple example in the US is the land that was taken from Native Americans and privatized. This privatization prevented indigenous people from the wealth and abundance of the land they used and cherished.

It is worth taking a serious look at the embedded values of the Free Market system, especially as we try to rebuild the rules in the aftermath of the recent global economic meltdown. Do the values and rules of our global economy reflect what you truly value? Is your outer world showing what your inner world yearns for? In what ways is our economic system life-affirming and in what ways is it life-diminishing? When we don't question the values entrenched in this system, we are silent enablers of the system. The more we think, talk and act to align our inner and outer world, the more pressure gets put on social structures and systems to shift.

As part of the World Expo held in Hanover Germany, Bill McDonough (mentioned earlier with his *Cradle to Cradle* book) proposed the Hanover Principles as a guiding set of values to shift the current paradigm. His principles addressed the inherent link between the spirit world and the physical world. Indigenous cultures around the globe have understood this for centuries. Most of those in power, and those of us who accept the current economic paradigm, have forgotten this. McDonough is quite effective in showing that if we don't pay attention to how we design our business products and factories, we have a strategy and design by default that will destroy us. He urges us to stop the "strategy of tragedy" and shift it to a "strategy of change and hope."

Businesses understand the power and use of money through consumer purchases and investments. You have more power than you think to shape the business practices of many firms. The recent growth of people buying foods more locally from farmer's markets and co-ops shows what happens when people vote with their wallet. Many national grocery stores now have sections called "local produce" and at least pay lip service to support local farmers. From executive compensation to environmental impact to fair labor practices, consumers make a difference in how businesses do business. Your money matters not only to you but to businesses around the globe.

Here are some simple steps to increasing your awareness of the power of your money:

1. Write a letter to one company that you usually purchase from and ask them what their policies are for purchasing supplies from companies that use sweat shops.

2. Email or call your pension fund and ask them about the labor, environmental, social practices of the firms they invest in.

3. Do a web search to find out if your favorite brand product is made by a company that is a member of Business for Social Responsibility or Social Venture Network.

4. Ask the grocery store chain where you shop whether they supply food products from farmers within a 50 mile radius of your town.

Prosperity vs. Poverty Consciousness—Money as Energy

Each of us determines where and towards whom our energy is directed, consciously or not. There is a spiritual principle, "Energy flows where attention goes." The more you understand the flow of energy in your life, the more consciously you align your material and spiritual world. Money, as a tool for aligning your inner and outer world, is one currency of energy. Examine all the ways you either block or allow energy to flow in your life. Through this self-examination you'll begin to see how much your life is based on a scarcity/ lack mindset vs. a prosperity/abundance mindset.

Every day you block energy flowing in your life or let it move freely to you and on to others. Your mindset, attitudes and beliefs determine how well you receive and let energy flow in your life. You can affirm that you already have what you need or worry about not getting what you need. You can give thanks for the blessings that are already in your life or you can believe that you don't have enough. Your consciousness (your awareness, attitudes, beliefs) all direct the flow of energy in your life.

As you focus your consciousness on abundant and limitless thinking, you will send more abundant energy into your world. Some people who have plenty of money still worry about having enough. Others with little money share what meager amounts they have with others. The difference between having a poverty mindset vs. a prosperity mindset is a belief in a loving, caring, abundant universe. Divine Presence is unlimited and abundant. Therefore, the energy of the universe is unlimited and abundant. Our job is to stay open to receiving that abundant energy and letting it flow effortlessly from us.

> *As you focus your consciousness on abundant and limitless thinking, you will send more abundant energy into your world.*

One of the spiritual laws for manifesting is, "What you give comes back three fold." Just as your heart pumps blood through your body by pushing blood into and out of the heart, you keep the flow of energy flowing through your life by both giving and receiving energy. By giving your energy in loving, joyful ways the best you can, you raise your life energy. As you have more life energy, you have more to share. Thus the cycle of giving and receiving continues, leading to more flow of love, joy, and other inner riches.

When you give attention to the love, joy and harmony that flows through your life you don't feel impoverished. Too often we look to the outer world to fulfill our inner world, but often it is just the opposite. When you have a rich inner life you'll find you have less need for as much riches in your outer world or you'll become less attached to the riches of the outer world. Richness in any form is all about energy. If you increase your sense of gratitude and acceptance of life as it occurs and don't struggle against it, you'll find that you experience more energy.

Some people hold poverty consciousness regardless of the amount of money or material goods they possess. They simply don't believe there is 'enough' in their life. This 'lack' mentality often drives them to act out of self-protection and fear of losing what they have. If they never perceive they have enough, they feel lack, and probably disappointment, resentment, anger or despair. That then lowers their life energy and they have to exert more energy to get what they want. Thus their life energy spirals downward.

You change the flow of energy in your life through your thoughts, words and deeds. What do you say or do that limits what you receive? How do you prevent energy or abundance from flowing? Reframing poverty and richness as more than financial or material goods, you recognize that prosperity and abundance comes in many forms. Giving thanks for all the blessings you have helps shift your awareness towards abundance.

When you shift your poverty consciousness, you will see a shift in the energy on the physical plane as well. It is often your own level of consciousness that keeps you stuck materially. Watch out for when you use phrases or self talk with messages such as "I can't do that" or "I don't deserve that." Make it a part of your spiritual practice to pay attention to how you describe your life with respect to prosperity, abundance, lack, poverty, financial success, or money. Notice next time you say, "I don't have enough . . . ." or "I can't afford . . . ." Turn that around and affirm that you have many blessings in your life. See how your energy shifts with that affirmation. Another practice is to give something in a loving manner to someone without expecting anything in return and see what flows into your life as a result. Do this as a small experiment to test the truth of these ideas.

> *Notice next time you say, "I don't have enough . . . ." or "I can't afford . . . ."*

Like a hose that expands as water flows through it, the more you expand your giving, the more you open your abundance hose. Tithing and providing your time and money to others expands your hose and allows more to flow through. The key is to not stay attached to the energy or abundance that flows. Simply let money and abundance come to you and move on to others through your acts of kindness and giving. You also have to be willing to receive energy from others. If you continually reject gifts offered such as time, support, money, or love, you shut off this flow of energy.

I've found that when I focus my intention and energy on my spiritual practice, more energy flows in my life. More often than not, I experience some serendipity or assistance that shifts my outer world in a beneficial way. It's up to me to stay open to receive that abundance and recognize the form the abundance takes.

Make a commitment to offer your energy as a gift to others. Incorporate into your spiritual practice some intentional offer of love through your talent or time in some way every day. You create a rich life in the process.

Using Money vs. Money Using You

You need energy in the form of calories for your physical body to stay alive. Yet there are empty calories and there are beneficial calories. Alcohol and refined sugar provide empty calories that don't sustain health over time. They taste good in the moment, but as a long term diet they do damage. So too money can be used in healthy ways to support your inner and outer world or not. Money can serve you in healthy ways such as to achieve balance in your life, or it can serve as a trap for greater consumption or help you run away from your deeper problems.

The voluntary simplicity movement from the 1990s focused attention on the role money plays in work-life balance. It has emerged again with the economic meltdown of 2008-09. This movement began in part by Joe Dominguez and Vicki Robin's book, *Your Money or Your Life: Transforming your Relationship with Money and Achieving Financial Independence.* Their book and workshops help you examine how you invest your life energy to create the kind of life you want.

Cynics have argued that the voluntary simplicity movement is merely the antidote for conspicuous consumption. Perhaps the latest global recession is the impetus for middle and upper class Americans to re-examine how much stuff (houses, cars, toys) they really need. Contrasting the voluntary simplicity movement are the challenges facing the working poor and lower class who work minimum wage jobs. In the bestseller book, *Nickel and Dimed,* Barbara Ehrenreich documented the hardships of the working poor. She gave voice to their plight, which is often ignored by main stream media.

With the economic meltdown of 2008 both the middle class and the working poor felt the pain of job shortages and making ends meet. The banking and investment decisions that supported short term payoffs, without respect to the larger damage they created, rippled across every social class. This changing economic climate is a unique opportunity for people to examine deeply the role money plays in their life.

Do you spend your time and energy truly living rather than chasing after money alone? Do you pay attention to how you are living without letting money dominate your life? Pay attention to your inner world and how that inner richness is brought into your outer world. Your inner richness adds fuel for your awakened soul journey. Balance and lasting happiness comes from feeding your spiritual life. Your values and inner harmony then guide your decisions and behaviors in your outer material world.

The beauty of *Your Money or Your Life* is that it provides an opportunity for people to examine how they use money rather than feeling powerless over their money It helps to look deeper at the desire and appeal for newness. Do you think if you have the latest greatest stuff, your life will be better? It comes back to examining what is truly valuable to you. How do you use money or other means to obtain what is valuable? The rise of websites such as FreeCycle and Craig's list and more second-hand stores, provide options for reusing things rather than spending more money for something new.

A law of economics says that as people's income rises so will their lifestyle. One reason is that people strive for more to fulfill needs and desires. It could be that humans are greedy, opportunistic beings, and their hunger never will be satisfied. Yet that kind of hell is self-imposed and can be turned around when one makes conscious choices about time and energy.

Much of the draw to buy new things comes from wanting something shiny and polished. But such a desire often stems from feelings of self worth. Do you feel better about yourself by the new material things you have in your life, or can you create a rich inner world irrespective of whether you have the latest gadget? There's prestige in getting the latest gizmo as soon as it comes off the market. If the gizmo is something that you highly value, then go for it. But if you have to buy the latest thing to fill a void in your inner world, look more closely within.

Many people shop to feel good, sometimes called "retail therapy". They have a rough week or something happens at work and they just want to buy something to have something fun to play with or new to look at. And that's probably healthier than going out and drinking a lot or having a one-night sexual encounter. But if the shopping is done in response to long term pain or inner wound, perhaps the money could be put to better use.

Money itself is value-free. What we use the money for shows what we value and demonstrates who we are. Look to see how money is a tool for your inner and outer world. A rich inner life used to strengthen a rich outer life of service, community, and harmonious relationships makes for lasting happiness and peace. I've heard that the Navajo considered the person who knew the most songs to be the richest one in the tribe. What kind of richness do you want to create in your life?

End of Chapter Exercises

1. What did money represent in your family growing up? What messages were you given as a child about money?

2. Was money used as control between your mother and father, or between adults and children? Was money hoarded or shared freely? How was an allowance determined—did you have to work for it or was it given without strings attached?

3. What were you taught about your worth based on money? Do you generally use materials things to establish your value to the world?

4. How were gifts given in your family? Was money used to show you were loved? How were other things done to show that people loved you (or didn't love you)?

5. Who makes decisions about money in your current immediate family? How are these decisions made? Is there input or discussion about how purchases are made?

CHAPTER 8

ꙮ

Working Spiritually

A bird does not sing because it has an answer.
A bird sings because it has a song.

Maya Angelou

In my book, *"Path for Greatness: Work as Spiritual Service,"* I focused on several important issues related to working spiritually. I'd like to just summarize here some of the key points and then move further into some areas where people requested more information or ideas.

A whole chapter was dedicated to explaining the difference between spirituality and religion. This distinction is particularly important to understand so that you and others feel comfortable talking about spirituality in the workplace, and to shift the focus away from religion at work. The media has covered Christian CEOs and their interest in running their business with a Christian focus. The coverage of spirituality at work needs to distinguish spirituality from religion, and explore the universal qualities of spirituality. Interested parties can read more on this in my earlier book.

In my workshops and talks about spirituality at work, I ask the audience to list all the words that describe spirituality or a spiritual experience. They frequently generate 40-50 words, such as joy, inner peace, compassion, balance, contentment, clarity, authenticity, etc. I like doing this exercise because it gets at universal ideas that cut across all religions. Thus spirituality at work applies to everyone regardless of their religious or cultural background.

This is a wonderful exercise because it not only makes the point that spirituality and religion are different, but it also eliminates people's fear that if they are spiritual at work they might offend someone. In fact, I point out just the opposite. Who wouldn't want to work in a workplace where people feel joy, compassion, balance, inner peace? We need to create more spiritual work environments, not shy away from spirituality at work. My approach is to have people see that spirituality at work is about honoring their own or others' wholeness and having everyone share their gifts authentically.

I use a flower as the metaphor for working spiritually. The starting point for a spiritually rich life comes from your spiritual soil. You must till your spiritual soil so that your ground is clear and nourished. From this soil grows your roots, which represents your purpose in life. When your roots are deeply planted, no matter how stormy the weather, you can still keep hold and not get toppled over. With a clear purpose, it's easier to make career and other life decisions. You create your life by design to live "on-purpose", and recognize when you are out of alignment with your soul's unfolding purpose.

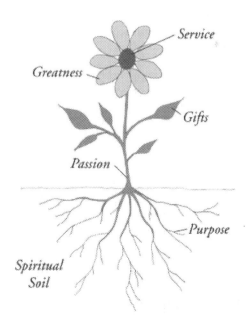

From those roots grows the stem of the plant, which is your passion. You live with passion and have greater energy for what you are doing when your purpose is clear. If you've ever met someone who has a clear purpose, you know how passionate and committed they are to their purpose. Out of the stem (passion) grow the leaves which are the gifts that you have to offer the world. When you are in alignment with your purpose and passion, your gifts can expand and feed your purpose. All this is done to offer yourself in service to others. When you offer service authentically, you blossom into the magnificence of who you are. The petals of the flower represent your greatness and beauty from living authentically.

In this chapter I'd like to explore how to work spiritually when you <u>know</u> you are a spiritual being on a spiritual journey. From this vantage point you can reframe how you work and why you are here. Those of you who have awakened to your soul journey, you already have made a commitment to use your work life to share your gifts and help others in that process as well.

Your soul journey takes place at work as much as in any other domain of life, particularly because you spend most of your waking hours at work. Too many people find themselves working in toxic work environments or unhealthy organizations. Learning how to navigate

> *Your soul journey takes place at work as much as in any other domain of life*

through such conditions and/or knowing when to leave requires careful spiritual discernment. Your work life offers you tremendous opportunity to practice your spiritual truths.

Here's a visualization you can use.

> *Imagine your colleagues as soul beings. See them as pure light in some form . . . . Greet them by name and thank them for being part of your work. Affirm that you are each there for a purpose to help one another . . . Imagine them each being surrounded in a gold or bright colored light. Send them energy and thoughts of joy, care, compassion. Send them on their way with the thought that they are a perfect expression of who they came here to be.*

It may be hard to fathom working spiritually because so often you are in the middle of conflicts or disagreements at work. Working spiritually doesn't mean that you walk around in a blissful state all the time. In fact sometimes the most spiritual thing you can do is pray for strength to endure until you can see your way out of a situation. Spirituality at work involves diligence, patience, and clarity as much as compassion, authenticity, and forgiveness. If you are bothered by someone's action, you need to consider what hot button is getting triggered for you. One spiritual practice is to be honest with your feelings and speak your truth with compassion and wisdom. The bottom line (figuratively and literally) is to remain open to your soul's unfolding and be intentional about dealing with your own stuff in the midst of chaos and conflict. Recognize too that others are also soul beings on their own path. That's the *spiritual work* that needs to be done in addition to any job assignments you're given from your boss. And it's just as important work to do.

Remember that you are exactly where you need to be to live out the spiritual journey you came to experience. Step in to it, celebrate it. Rejoice in being the bright beautiful being that you are. We work as spiritual beings through our heart, mind, and hands. Or as Kahlil Gibran more eloquently wrote, "When you work, you are a flute, through whose heart the whispering of the hours turns to music."

My previous book focused on the new versus old paradigms for organizations (see chapters 16 & 17 in *Path for Greatness*). As organizations move more toward team work, decentralized decision making, and empowerment, more conflict and miscommunication are likely to arise. The old style command and control has its advantages because there is one person (or one group) making decisions. They issue orders or pass down decrees that others are supposed to follow. However, you have to learn new ways of relating to each other as you're shifting away from these old control-based models of managing.

In today's economy, businesses have to be far more responsive and flexible to handle change and innovation. Old command and control styles don't allow the nimbleness needed today and diminishes employee emotional and spiritual health. Domination and 'leader-knows-all' leadership style simply won't work in today's fast paced global economy. It similarly reduces employee engagement, creativity and motivation, which ultimately diminishes productivity and performance.

Applying Spiritual Principles to Workplace Problems

Too many typical problems arise in the workplace to offer any sort of cookbook approach on how to handle them. I'll address the main ones where spirituality can apply. Obviously good communication, teamwork, and interpersonal skills are essential for working through conflicts, personality clashes, personal agendas and stylistic differences. From a spiritual perspective, you can view these challenges as the arena for your spiritual unfolding, and opportunities to deepen your spiritual practice. Can you view the other players in the scene as the actors and props for your spiritual progression?

Personal Dramas and Shadow Work:

One reason you get off balance at work is that you are constantly dealing not only with uncertainty of job projects and deadlines but also with other people's energy. Far too many people are off-center or have wobbly energy. Their energy is just swirling around and isn't grounded. Thus they come crashing into you and others at work. It's like an energy cyclone blowing through. Anyone can get sucked up in the energy swirl. It helps to know how to stay grounded in the midst of that swirl.

Pay attention to when you get caught in someone else's drama. Many dramas get created at work: people not believing they are listened to, not feeling appreciated, being overworked, needing more respect, feeling insecure, feeling powerless, needing to assert their power or will, etc. Whatever the drama is, stay open to it being just that—a drama. You can decide how much to get hooked into it. Sometimes you are forced to deal with the drama if it involves a co-worker, client, supervisor or direct reports.

A spiritual truth that has really helped me move through blocks and barriers is "Energy flows where attention goes". What and to whom are you directing attention in your work? How are you feeding energy into people and systems that are working? Are you putting a lot of energy into systems or people who are toxic? Notice what draws your attention and time during the course of a day. Have you taken the time to show gratitude for something that was done well? Have you taken the time to cultivate good relations with others? Pay attention to what you give your energy to and see if there aren't some shifts you can make. Will you feed the dramas with your energy or will you put your energy into life affirming and spiritually renewing activities? Choose to focus your own energy on constructive supportive activities more than others' problems or personal dramas.

You can feed someone's belief of victimhood, inadequacy, confusion, insecurity, etc. if you are not careful. Do you find yourself stepping in to "fix" other people's problems? Do people often share their 'ain't it awful' stories with you? Notice when you get hooked into playing the hero or the victim in such situations. If you feel you must be the hero and save the day, you will take on the responsibility of helping straighten someone else's mess. In playing the hero, they do not learn to clean-up their own mess. Having a formal role of supervisor means you have to attend to employee performance and sometimes personal struggles. Yet you can do that through coaching questions that allows the employee to find her own answers rather than you stepping in to 'fix them'. If you feel you need to be a hero to help save the day, check your own motives for this. What are you trying to get out of the drama with this other person?

If you feel it is your duty to set others straight so they see things your way, you will be setting yourself up for resistance and further dramas. If you feel you need to teach someone a lesson or block their power moves, you also will get resistance and likely will escalate whatever drama is unfolding.

If you find yourself fearful or defensive at work, what inner strength and wisdom can you draw upon to bolster your confidence and self assurance? Think of something simple you can do to reconnect to your Divine Essence or any spirit guides you have. Some people keep little angel figurines or Buddha statues or pictures of holy shrines to remind them of their Spiritual Source. This will help shift your energy from fear to unlimited compassion, mercy, strength and hope. Your awakened energy will shift the situation at hand. As in a dance, if even one person's energy and attitude changes, the other dancers are affected. They then have to shift accordingly.

What spiritual practice can you use to remove your blocks and be a clear channel for your Higher Power to move through you? Find ways or people at work to remind you to respond with compassion rather than criticism. Take time each day to cultivate your spiritual soil so that when you get into turmoil at work, you will be able to respond more easefully and with greater grace. When you get your hot buttons pushed, stay open to seeing what lesson is being offered for your growth and learning, rather than react defensively.

Pay attention as well to when your personal agenda or ego gets in the way of making a relationship work smoothly. Early in my career I got an important insight regarding this issue that I have revisited over the years. I kept getting frustrated at an intern I supervised because she did not listen to my advice or what I suggested she do. She was quite bright so I gave her a lot of running room. However, there were times when she wasn't sure what to do and didn't take my advice. I felt some obligation in my role to help mentor and guide her, but she would have none of it. I felt frustrated that I wasn't fulfilling my role with the intern and also concerned about her work. I also took it as a personal insult that she wasn't listening to me. That was my hook that kept getting pulled. She paid attention to my boss but ignored my input.

It wasn't until the very end of her time with us that I realized how personally I was taking things. Rather than see it as <u>her</u> learning experience to get as much or little out of the internship as she could, I felt slighted and somewhat belittled by her. She triggered my button about not being taken seriously, and I reacted from that place. My insight was that *you can't teach people who aren't open to learning*. Once I got this insight, I backed off from trying to teach her anything. My boss noticed my change of behavior fairly quickly and asked about it. I told him that if the intern wasn't open to learning from me it wasn't worth my energy trying to make her learn.

I could continue to be frustrated or just let her take from the internship what she wanted. It no longer was an ego thing for me, and therefore I didn't continue the dance of one-ups-manship we had been doing. That was very freeing.

Pay attention to when you find yourself thinking "poor me, pity me". Playing out this victim mentality only keeps you stuck and feeling helpless. Figure out when you <u>do</u> have power and what you can do differently, then work on that. It may be a time for you to practice letting go of old beliefs about others that you don't need to hold onto anymore. You may be getting some deeper issues triggered around your self-worth or competency.

If you catch yourself thinking you are somehow a victim in your workplace, consider how you may have given your power away. Have you not set clear boundaries with someone? Are you afraid to assert your opinion or challenge someone else's thoughts? Do you shy away from confronting people because you are a conflict avoider? All these behaviors perpetuate problems that, in fact, you have the power to address—if you claim your power and courage to do so.

If you are in the middle of a drama at work, see what is being presented to deepen your spiritual practice. Assume the person is bringing you a gift in this situation and try to determine what it is. This will help you avoid believing you are a victim of other people's dramas. When you can find the gift in the situation, you can shift out of the victim mentality and affirm your power to move through the situation more effectively.

In some situations we don't have "ears to hear or eyes to see." If you can't determine how to handle the situation, ask your spirit guides to show you another way of seeing the situation. You may need a friendly nudge to open your eyes to see what is happening for your own or someone else's conscious evolution to take place. Talking things over with a job coach or an EAP counselor if your company has this available, can help you see things in a different light. Even if you can't change the other person's behavior, it is still possible for you to find a way to see the situation differently. It may take time to get this clarity and you may need some distance from the situation. At a minimum, accept that this situation allows you to practice patience, compassion, and greater understanding.

I've done some coaching work with employees who get caught up in each other's dramas. None of them like the tension, yet they are afraid to confront the behaviors when they occur. They wait for someone else, usually a supervisor or consultant, to step in and address the issues. I encourage them to claim their own power rather than shift the responsibility for others to deal with a problem. Once we discuss some constructive confrontation methods, I encourage them to practice over the next week a different way of responding. It is scary at first to change the drama dance at work. Yet over time and with practice, they usually find better strategies for dealing with the issue than ignoring it or waiting for their supervisor to step in. Sometimes a mediator or neutral person is needed to provide safe space to practice the skills to make the behavior changes stick.

Remind yourself there is a bigger scenario being played out than you can see at this time. Many situations are provided specifically for you to shift how you respond to things. You can learn how to shift the drama dance now, or you can keep dancing it with the same or new people. Practice compassion with yourself as well. It takes time to learn new ways of responding. Stay open in a spirit of allowing, not resisting what needs to happen next nor forcing a specific outcome. This is hard work but vital to your spiritual progression.

Energy Vampires:

Other kinds of dramas at work can include people bringing their personal crises to work and dumping them on the table for all to hear. Sometimes people's personal lives do impact work and you need to attend to it. In fact some of your greatest spiritual moments at work may be spent listening to a co-worker through a difficult time and supporting them as they work through it.

Beware of energy vampires. They suck you dry because they can never get enough attention or sympathy. Energy vampires go to those sympathetic people who are willing to listen to their sob story. If you feel continually drained by someone who constantly comes to you with their sob story, you may very well need to set up greater boundaries with them. Either verbally or mentally set your determination that you aren't going to be part of their pity party. Consciously affirm their Divine Essence even if they can't see it in themselves.

If a co-worker complains to others or continues to dump out his sob story, then try to find a song or mantra to repeat so that you don't listen as much. If he suffers aloud or on the phone, visualize a white light washing over him so that his pain can be removed in the best possible way for all concerned. You may need to say something so he knows his drama is affecting other people's ability to get their work done. Remind him that he can do things to change his life and encourage him to take positive steps in that direction. Maybe the best thing you can do is to remind your co-worker that he doesn't have to see himself as a victim. Again you will need to be centered when you do this so your words are ones of compassion rather than judgments or criticism. If you come from compassion, your co-worker is more likely to hear you. If you come from a place of condemnation, you'll only increase his pain, defensiveness or resistance.

Here is a visualization you can use to protect yourself or help set healthy boundaries from energy vampires.

> *Imagine a bubble of white, gold or bright colored light surrounding you. Affirm that this light will sustain you and replenish your energy. Ask that the bubble around you deflects energy that isn't in your highest good. Ask that you be able to be present to the other person in healthy ways and that you are able to affirm their highest good in ways that also work for you.*

Do this visualization as many times during the course of the day that you need to remind yourself that you and the other are Divine Beings on a soul journey.

Another technique to clear your energy is to imagine wiping away the energy of the person after she has been in your presence. You can wave your hand around your body and say "I release all negative and unnecessary energy of this person" or "I no longer stay attached to this person's energy and do not allow it to be part of my energy field consciously or non-consciously." Then you can mentally scan your office or area and visualize it being filled with healing light. Consciously call in the energy you desire for your highest good. If the conditions are right, smudge your office or workspace with incense, sage or use aroma therapy to cleanse the energy in the room. You can also use water-based sprays or light scented spritzers for this same purpose.

When I facilitate a meeting that I think could be tense, before the meeting I visualize the room being infused with healing energy. I see it filled with light and then ask that the highest good be done by and with all parties involved. During the course of the meeting I'll connect my Divine Expression with members' Higher Power and affirm that they will speak or act from that Source. Such visualizations and affirmations are powerful ways to get into right alignment mentally and energetically before a potentially turbulent situation results. You also can ask for your angel or spirit guides to assist you during the course of a difficult meeting or encounter.

Our work environments are just stews of energy brewing. Each person's energy field affects the energy fields around them and so chain reactions happen all the time. Most of the time, groups know how to keep the pot from boiling over. Yet sometimes it needs a major eruption to get people focused on the issues at hand. There's only so much you can do about someone who needs greater healing. They may or may not be ready to do their healing work. If you're fortunate, your co-workers are dealing with their issues and taking steps to get back into balance. The more common case is that they don't even realize how out of balance they are or how they are bringing their woundedness to their workplace. And it rarely is just one person out of balance at work. Your patience, care and support can help ground the energy in your workplace so it doesn't spiral out of control or become too out of balance.

Power Trips:

Other problems to deal with are power trips and control games. Some people may not be aware they use intimidation to get their way. Yet anyone who questions them could be a target for retaliation. It is natural to want to have power and control over your life, to be effective in managing your world. The crucial issue is how you use power and control. Do you use power <u>over</u> others or power *with* others? Power and control games are really good examples of the shadow at work because we all play our games at one time or another.

> *Do you use power <u>over</u> others or power with others?*

If you shy away from confronting someone who is walking all over you and you resent being taken advantage of, why are you afraid of claiming your power? Dealing with your fears helps you remove the hook of other people's actions. When you feel fear emerge in a situation, take time to discern what this fear is showing you about you. It's no one else's job but your own to clear your fears. Know you are supported in this process simply by asking your Higher Power to assist you. *"Help me do Thy will Great Spirit/Allah/Yaweh."*

People don't try to control others unless there is something they want and fear they won't get it. If they are using power and manipulation to get something, it usually means they are living in lack-consciousness which ultimately is about fear. You may sense you are in the direct line of a wrecking ball in this instance and need to duck. Applying some of the same elements as martial arts can be very useful. Step aside while re-directing their energy and disarming them. Practice allowing others' comments to move past you without hooking you into a conflict. If your typical response is to push back, take a deep breath and figure out what you need to feel safe. Learn how to move around the other's attempts to upset you by seeing and hearing them with the eyes and ears of compassion.

Here is a visualization you can use to work with power from a spiritual base:

> *Imagine a cone of energy surrounding yourself and the other people who are engaged in a power trip. This cone points down to Mother Earth to ground your energy. This cone connects you and them to Mother Earth. Breathe deeply and draw energy up from Mother Earth. Imagine the energy as a gold or yellow light. Visualize yourself and the others filled with this energy . . . .*
>
> *Now imagine another cone extending from you and the others up towards Father Sky. Breathe deeply and draw down energy to you so that this energy fills you and the others. Visualize this energy as a violet color. Now have the violet energy light meet the gold energy light in your heart . . .*
>
> *Breathe deeply for 3 deep breaths pulling the energy up from Mother Earth and down from Father Sky meeting in your heart center.*
>
> *Affirm that you and the others in your situation now have all the energy they need. You and they no longer need to engage in power struggles to get energy because you have all the energy you are seeking. You and they can now breathe together the powerful force of Nature to act harmoniously in all situations. This flow of energy and power comes to you easily as you breathe in and out, intentionally drawing in Source Energy. Feel how you are now filled with love, peace, and balance . . .*

Pay attention to your defense mechanisms and what fears get triggered for you. Watch when you get hooked emotionally and remember that you can't control or change the other person. You can side-step others' unbalanced energy or do the above or similar visualizations to help ground the energy. You'll find that the more you clear out your own emotional wounds and self-doubts, the less you'll need to defend yourself. Focus on your own strength and Source Energy so you can deal with whatever conditions you face. You can always surrender the situation to Divine Wisdom. As Richard Bach reminds us in his book *Illusion*, "The River delights to set us free as long as we dare let go."

We're Operating on God Time

American society is so geared to 24-7 access that taking time to breathe in silence or unplug for a day may feel un-natural. You may find it challenging to bring your fast paced life back into balance. It helps to follow natural rhythms of action and inaction, work and rest. Neglecting the natural ebbs and flows of energy, you run the risk of burning out. We are seeing the serious consequences of our frantic lifestyles on planet earth. As one bumper sticker reads: "Nature bats last." This reminds us that we humans can't control everything. As much as we might like to think otherwise, we operate on God time and the rhythms of Nature.

I believe the desire to stay connected 24-7 comes in part from fear: fear you will be left behind, fear you won't be successful, fear of how others will perceive you if you aren't instantaneously accessible. Of course the marketing geniuses play on that fear. Yet you have a secret weapon that you can use as an antidote. It is your belief that *All is in Divine Right Order*. This belief helps you be more patient for the greater mystery to unfold. Affirming that you have all that you need, trusting in Divine Right Order to unfold, you then regulate and monitor the energy you send to the Universe. You don't need to panic or respond from fear. Instead allow and connect to Divine Wisdom to understand what is yours to do next.

Over the years I've learned that I can't see the whole picture, and that things don't operate on <u>my</u> time frame. I keep getting reminders to surrender my agenda when events don't follow according to my plan. Slowly I've learned to stay open to something bigger unfolding.

Here's just a small example of how this can happen. When I left one job I had packed up everything in my office in a fairly organized fashion so I could find things later. A couple months later working on a different project, I looked for a folder that I thought I had put in the properly marked box but couldn't find it anywhere. I looked in all the other boxes I had packed and couldn't find *any* of the folders for that project. I then looked for the disks where the file could be retrieved. Despite being careful to put those disks in a noticeable place, they were nowhere to be found.

I was starting to get frustrated and mad at myself for not having packed things as well as I thought I had. I calmed down and located a CD that I had burned from earlier and thought, "Whew, at least I can get to the file with this CD." When I went to open the folders from the CD, I got an error message on my computer saying the files wouldn't open! By this time I was getting really frustrated because I needed to send the document that afternoon. Rather than panic, I called technical support at my old job to see what was up with the CD. Our computer technician said that sometimes those types of CDs are finicky on certain machines but if I went to her office to get another type of CD she would help me transfer the files. While I felt more confident I would get the file printed and mailed in time, I was intrigued at why so many of my back-up plans had failed. I let it go and figured there was another reason for this extra delay and effort.

On my way to see the technical support person, I stopped to see my previous secretary, a wonderful, sweet woman. She told me that she was retiring at the end of the month. I was really surprised by that since she didn't mention it to me before I left my job a few weeks earlier. I wished her well in her retirement and we talked about what she was planning on doing. It occurred to me leaving the secretary's office that if I hadn't gone to see the tech support person, I would have never been able to say goodbye to this secretary and wish her well. Since we had been close while I worked there, I was so glad I had that opportunity to thank her for all her years working there.

The lesson for me over the years has been that even when we do our best to make things happen smoothly they don't always go as planned. In those instances rather than banging my head against the wall, I need to take a deep breath and see what else is unfolding. Now when such frustrations happen I try to stay open for whatever else needs to happen. In my best moments I remember to say, "Wow I can't wait to see what Spirit is going to do with this." On good days I get the bigger picture within hours. The paradox of living as a spiritual being in the physical world gets resolved by seeing the opportunity for joy, love and abundance in all situations. The key is remembering to stay open to Divine Presence and allowing Source Energy to flow through the situation in wonderful and unexpected ways.

Acceptance as Spiritual Practice

As much as we would like to be perfect or have others live up to our expectations, they often don't and we aren't perfect either. Acceptance of your own and others' frailties helps to shift from condemnation or anger to compassionate understanding. You won't spend nearly as much time trying to fix someone else, but rather appreciate the gifts they offer in the moment.

If you continually judge people based on their worst behavior, you never get past your own filters. Hold the thought that your co-workers are whole and wonderful. Affirm that others are capable of solving their own problems, changing how they react or learning from their behaviors. See them as bright beautiful spiritual beings, even if they don't display it in the moment. Shifting expectations of others can do wonders in how they react to you differently. As any teacher will tell you, the self-fulfilling prophecy holds true. If you expect someone to act out, usually they will. If you see them as a wonderful being doing their best to live in the world, you'll connect with them more compassionately. They will pick up on your supportive energy and frequently change how they react.

A colleague taught me this expression that I've remembered over the years, "You are the perfect expression of who you are at this moment in time. *You can be nothing other than that.*" Accepting people as they are and looking for the gifts they bring, yields far greater results than being upset that others aren't living up to your expectations of them. It is hard when you are supervised by someone less skilled than you, but there may be a lesson in there for you on patience or tolerance. Rather than stewing in your frustration at someone else's incompetence, especially if there is nothing you can do about it, remind yourself, "We're all doing the best job we can at any moment." I also like this quote: "Have patience with me, God isn't done with me yet." What a great reminder that we are all a work in progress!

When you get frustrated with someone else who seems to learn their lessons more slowly, look back at times when it took you several dozen or several hundred attempts to master an important life skill or spiritual lesson. Honor and bless others' journeys as you do your own. Find patience and forgiveness as deeply as you can in that moment and let the rest go. Staying attached to your anger doesn't do you or anyone else any good. If you can find ways to help the person learn some skill they seem to be lacking, then provide that assistance. Remember, it will be up to each person to receive help as they are ready to shift out of their past patterns. You can't teach someone who isn't ready to learn.

Spiritual Centering

Many people don't set aside time for spiritual centering. This is such valuable time. Time Out is Time Invested. Rather than seeing it as time away from other important things, shift your perspective and see that it adds to your life. Notice how much more easily your day flows with a clear head and calm heart. Most people can't imagine going a day without brushing their teeth. So too will your day feel complete with regular time spent on your spiritual practice.

Even if you can't take 30 minutes from your day to pray, meditate or reflect in silence, you can use your lunch break to find ways to quiet your mind. On your commute to or from work you can listen to calming music, chanting, or other meditative media. 'First Things First' means putting your Higher Power in front of all the other tasks you need to complete in your day.

There are many simple breathing techniques for clearing your mind and focusing on your Higher Power. Perhaps you have a favorite quote or inspirational passage. Keep that handy so you can refer to it throughout the day. One breathing technique I use to help me focus on my breath and tune into the present moment is from Thich Nhat Hanh: "Breathing in I calm my body, Breathing out I smile." While you say the words on the in-breath, relax your jaws, face, arms, shoulders. Smile broadly on the out-breath. Even the simple act of smiling will help you shift your energy and focus. For more in-depth meditation or spiritual centering practices, consider doing a retreat at a monastery or meditation center, or take a workshop at a yoga center, church, temple or mosque. Prayer beads or short mantras offer focal points for the wandering mind.

Here are some useful techniques for focusing and quieting your mind.

1. *Follow your breath as it comes through your nose and into your lungs and abdomen. Focus on the breath and feel it move through your body. Allow the breath to get steadier and slower. Visualize the breath bringing in new oxygen to your body and flowing down your arms and down into your feet. On the exhale, breath out whatever distracting thoughts or worries you are carrying in your body. Relax your body as you do this breath work and allow all thoughts to blow out with each breath.*

2. *Focus on the openings of your nostrils as the air flows in and out. Keep your focus on this space for five minutes, feeling the air pass through. Focus on the emptiness of the space. Let your mind expand into that emptiness. If a thought comes forward, release it with your exhale. Don't force your thoughts or your breathing but simply allow thoughts to float by as if riding on each breath. Keep your attention on the opening in your nostril. Relax and breathe.*

You will be surprised how quickly your mind can become still if you have a focal point and pay attention to your breathing. From this place of emptiness, listen for any guidance that comes your way. It may happen in the breathing or at a later time. The main thing is to empty yourself enough of your internal chatter to allow new insights and clarity to emerge.

I found early on in my process that guided meditations and retreats worked better for me than just sitting in silence. I needed more structure to learn how to be quiet. It's amazing how we learn to multitask 3,4,5 things at once. The "monkey mind chatter" fills our head easily. We forget what it is like to be quiet and observe the world like a small child. Through guided silent retreats with a seasoned spiritual director you can learn the nuances needed to calm your mind enough to hear and discern the call of Spirit. If there is an un-programmed Friends (Quaker) meeting in your area, you can go there to experience sitting in silence and learning how to listen for the still small voice of Spirit.

If you are a kinesthetic or more physical person, take a break from work for a quiet walk, exercise, tai chi, or yoga to focus on your breath and clear your mind. You may be a visually artistic person, so doing some sort of drawing or creating a mandala will help you clear your mind. If you are musically inclined, you may feel more calm and centered playing an instrument or listening to spiritually uplifting music.

One thing I do to help me stay grounded during the course of a busy or stressful day is to carry a stone in my pocket. I will often pick up stones from various places. They aren't usually fancy or colorful, but stones that get my attention or feel good in my hand. If I have a tough meeting to attend or think I may have a run-in with someone that I'm not looking forward to encountering, just holding the stone in my pocket or rubbing it for a few seconds helps me ground myself. The stone also reminds me to ask Spirit that the right highest good be done. I've given such stones to people who are going through tough times. Frequently I receive a thank-you from them days or weeks later saying the stone really helped them maintain their balance during that time. Prayer beads or other devotional objects also work for this.

For prolonged stressful situations or if your job is inherently stressful, professional support groups can be very helpful. If you don't know of a professional group related to your work, look for workshops that address spirituality and work. There has been an upsurge in workshops geared for business people to help them deal with their stress from a spiritual perspective. These groups may be run by clergy or lay people either during the day or after work.

If you don't know of such a group in your area, you may want to start one or ask a clergy or experienced person to help you organize one. Such sessions can be informal brown bag lunches or formal sessions where there is a program or reading to help people find some focus and balance.

If you can't get with a group of people for a regularly scheduled meeting, perhaps there are people you know who would be willing to be part of a spiritual support group for you. I have had co-workers request that I lead meditations over our lunch hour so they can calm their mind and deepen their practice. I did this on a regular basis for a while and then was on stand-by to assist whenever they really felt the stress was just too much. Find such people in your circle of friends who could provide this break in your day.

You may already subscribe to websites that offer inspirational stories or quotes. These are helpful to look at throughout the day. They often provide just the right thought to shift perspective. I write a weekly blog (found on my website www.lindajferguson.com) where you can read more on this topic. One website that offers meditations from various faith traditions is the 'Winter Feast for the Soul' website. They offer podcasts and videos that you can listen to throughout the day.

Other resources that might be available in your area include spiritual directors, spiritually oriented EAP counselors, or job/life coaches. The International Association of Spiritual Directors has a website with helpful information or you can find useful resources on my website "Coaching" page. Another resource is the Meet-Up website that shows groups in many locations; you can look for a spiritual group to discuss scripture, share rituals or ceremony, meditations, chanting, or other practices. Specific support groups, like grief support groups or Alcohol Anonymous, often hold meetings during the lunch hour to assist those who need extra help getting through their day.

As more and more people awaken and desire work that is more meaningful and fulfilling, there are more resources available than ever. Find the right group, leader or website that suits your needs. The important thing is to keep your spiritual soil fertile and nourished. When you are able to more easily connect with your Inner Wisdom, you'll find it easier to move through the stressors and challenges of your day.

When you hit times of stress and challenge, look at them as opportunities to strengthen your faith or spiritual practice. As Mother Teresa is quoted as saying: "God never gives us a task we are not up to. I just wish sometimes He didn't trust me so much." You are guided and supported in all that you do. Know it, feel it, believe it.

Your work provides a great opportunity to express your gifts in service to others. Work provides opportunities to share your beauty, gifts, passion and joy with others. Your soul journey continues through your work, as you express and understand your greater life purpose.

> *If you look to others you will never be truly fulfilled. If your happiness depends on money, you will never be happy with yourself.*
>
> *Be content with what you have, rejoice in the way things are. When you realize there is nothing lacking, the world belongs to you.*
>
> *Lao Tzu*

End of Chapter Exercises

1. How do you deal with other people's fears? What will help you stay grounded when someone explodes or gets visibly upset in front of you? What do you need to feel safe in this situation?

2. When you find yourself locked in a power struggle with someone, ask yourself:

    a. What about the other is hooking my power and control issues?

    b. What does this power struggle teach me about my own behavior? My soul journey?

    c. What do I still need to learn about using power? What do I need to learn about taking control of my life? Surrendering control?

    Visualize yourself cutting an energetic cord attached to this person. Imagine that you and s/he are dancing freely. Bless him as you step back, not connected to his energy any longer. You are free to be whole and creative, to express your Divine Essence as you feel it needs to be expressed.

    Repeat this visualization as many times as necessary until you can clearly see yourself free from any hooks or emotional attachments to this person now or in the future.

3. If you are continually bothered by someone in particular, ask yourself:

    a. What hot button is getting triggered inside me by this person?

    b. What do I need to see more clearly about myself?

    c. What will help me shift from anger or fear to joy, acceptance or compassion?

> *Visualize this person being filled with bright light, so that they glow with pulsing waves of love and radiant harmony. Feel those waves move out from you as well. Feel your workplace filled with the radiance of harmony and peace.*

Repeat this as many times as necessary until you can hold this image and feeling for three minutes.

CHAPTER 9

✿

Living in the Aquarian Era

Enlightened Beings have no castle walls to defend.

Peter Calhoun

The Emerging Aquarian Era

The major lesson of the Piscean era, the last two thousand years approximately, was to love others as you love yourself. This is the Golden Rule that has been taught in many traditions. While many souls are still learning this lesson, in the Aquarian era there is a new lesson to learn, one of wholeness and integration rather than separation. This new era involves a shift in understanding we are One. Therefore, the emerging Aquarian Era means moving away from separation thinking, you vs. me, to understanding we are all one body interconnected through Source Energy. Our souls unite in Universal Mind consciousness. Our ability to see that unity depends on our awareness that we are One. The emerging paradigm is to hold that awareness with your daily life, family, society, and the planet.

Energy is the driving force in the Aquarian Era, not products, nations, territory or money. As we learn to live more intentionally, working with Source energy, we know that there is no scarcity, no need to horde or control others to get what we want or need. We live joyfully and we draw in more energy to share with the world. When we shut down emotionally, get angry, act defensive etc., we close off the abundant energy flow. To generate more of what we need, we raise our vibrational frequency and draw down Source Energy. This is a dramatic paradigm shift of the new Aquarian era.

Many of the upheavals and transitions of the twentieth century are considered signs of a shift to a new era. The shift from the Piscean era to the Aquarian era began within the last hundred years. Few will deny the rapid shifts that occurred in the twentieth century. It began with two world wars, the magnitude of which had not been seen on the planet. Out of those events grew global initiatives, such as the United Nations, designed to foster greater collaboration. With the onset of satellites, air travel, and digital communication the world became increasingly more interconnected. The world-wide web (www) is a great demonstration of our inter-connection.

The end of the twentieth century saw the creation of wealth from the digital age, followed by the "dot-bomb" implosion, and then the global economic collapse of 2008-2009. What economic structures get rebuilt in the aftermath of the global recession will determine how we move forward collectively.

The past several decades brought progress in civil rights for people of color, women, and gays/lesbians. The collapse of the Soviet and Maoist regimes led to greater freedom and human rights. We are witnessing movement towards greater democracy in the Arab/Middle East countries as the twenty first century unfolds. Institutions that no longer serve the greater good of humanity are crumbling and need to be rebuilt.

The transition from the Piscean to the Aquarian era involved transformations of self-awareness and interdependence, along with cultural and technological breakthroughs around the globe. Jesus taught during the Piscean era to love your enemy. Now in the Aquarian Era, a critical lesson is to move past enemy images entirely and stop using language of us vs. them. The paradigm shift now is to understand the interconnected One-ness of all beings. The enemy is not the economic system, bankers, the government, the schools, or the churches. Poor people, homosexuals or people of different religions or ethnicities aren't an "other" to be oppressed or de-humanized. All these systems and groups are part of the tapestry of the One. Each has its part for the conscious evolution of us all.

Another critical task in this new emerging Aquarian era is to get back into harmony and balance with the earth. This involves understanding that the plants and animals are also part of the Holy Oneness. Indigenous people have held this truth and knowing over the centuries. The domination and colonization of Western culture over Earth-based cultures has broken the cords of sacred Oneness. The Western "advanced" cultures lost their connection with the earth, Her Wisdom, and relationship with all creatures. The Lakota expression, Mitakuye Oyasin, reminds us to pray and give thanks "to all my relations". Our calling now is to shift from the worldview of dominion over Nature to reclaim harmony and balance with Nature. Now is the time to Re-member our sacred connection to Mother Earth.

The new Aquarian era has brought forth greater self-expression but also more fear from those threatened by the change of the social order. For example, feminist theologians questioned patriarchal church doctrine and more women entered every profession. Power shifts occurred as those in dominant positions had to relinquish their social advantage and share power with multiple groups. Many pushed back or resisted these changes to keep the social order as it had been for centuries.

Cultural shifts in the Aquarian era means moving away from rigid adherence to systems that oppress. As was evident throughout the twentieth century, it takes strength, courage and determination to shift social structures. In the Aquarian era people and situations that are not authentic to Divine Expression of wholeness and Love will transform or dissolve. Shifts towards wholeness are happening more quickly personally and across the global landscape of politics and finance.

Emerging new Gender Identities of Wholeness

Our new era also ushers a change from entrenched gender roles to awareness and appreciation of balanced gender qualities. Certain qualities that have been categorized as "masculine" and "feminine" are more balanced in the Aquarian era.

Qualities often associated with the feminine are receptivity, allowing, flowing. Qualities often associated with the masculine are force, action and focus. "Female" characteristics such as intuition, expansiveness, creativity, and nurturing are necessary for healthy living regardless of one's gender. "Male" characteristics of determination and assertiveness are also important. When masculine qualities get out of balance, domination and power-over (rather than power-with) are used to get things accomplished. When feminine qualities of nurturance and receptivity are taken to the extreme and not balanced, burnout, co-dependency, or passivity prevail. Balance and integration is what is needed to thrive in the new era.

Greater synergy for daily living occurs by combining the masculine and feminine energies. Self-nurturing and nurturing for others, along with action and focus, support your daily life and the Holy Oneness. These qualities strengthen as you awaken your Divine Essence of joy, love, harmony and power.

In the Aquarian era there is less pressure to be masculine <u>versus</u> feminine, rather a recognition that *both* qualities are valuable and needed for greater harmony, on the personal and societal level. One's sexual orientation or gender identification matters less as the blending of masculine and feminine arises within individuals and within relationships. As we shift to a new era, the male and female energies are equally honored and appreciated.

Proper balance of these energies leads to healthier relationships. In this new era people learn to cultivate those qualities within themselves to manifest balance in their outer world. More people understand that they create their world from the inside out. This expands on the ancient Judeo-Christian teaching, "That which you sow, so shall you reap". What you sow on the inside, what you focus your attention on or energetically feed, you bring forth in the world. Thus, if you are out of balance you create turbulence in your relationships, your work, your health etc. As you integrate the masculine and the feminine, and become more whole, you experience the treasures of that balance in your inner and outer world. You show up as your grandest self, awakened to your Inner Radiance.

Integrating your life as a spiritual being in physical form, you mirror the beauty and wisdom of the Holy Oneness. Others mirror this as well, reflecting their radiance. As such, you may feel attracted to all sorts of people who have awakened to their spiritual path. You'll feel drawn to their energy, their etheric field, or your soul commitments with them. Don't get hung up on the fact that someone of a large age span or a different sexual orientation seems attractive. You are connecting at a soul level as much, or more so, than the human dimension. Step out of your past programming of how people need to show up in the world. Instead, reach out to them as the beautiful soul beings that they are.

Celebrate all the awakened beings you encounter. Rejoice in their beauty and their Light. May you create spiritually guided, loving relationships with all the people in your life. Alhamdulillah, Halelu Yah!

Remembering to call forth Source Energy

In the new era of understanding the Holy Oneness, our spiritual practice includes remembering we are not separate from Divine Creation. We are the hologram of Divine Essence. As soul beings we express Divine Essence naturally. It's only through social conditioning that many have forgotten. As you follow your awakened soul journey, it becomes easier to remember you are that expression of Love.

> *As soul beings we express Divine Essence naturally.*

Draw upon Spirit and bathe in the comfort of Love's grace daily. Doing so gives you strength and support to stay grounded in shifting sand. Your tendency may be to run for cover or shut down emotionally during a crisis or when stressed. This only blocks Source Energy from coming through you. Affirming Divine Essence as your true nature raises your energy. Greater flow of Source Energy supports your movement through challenges. Your life conditions then shift more easefully to greater harmony, balance, and peace. Remember you are Divine Essence as the acorn knows it's a mighty oak tree.

Source Energy is unlimited and accessible. It can neither be created nor destroyed. The key is in how you use it. Remind yourself in as many ways as necessary that you are a vessel for this Source Energy. Remember as well to call on your spirit guides, power animals, angels, or ancestors to support your journey.

Here is an affirmation to use as a daily reminder of our Divine Essence:

> *I am a Divine Expression of pure Love. I allow and welcome Loving Divine Energy to pulse through me at this very moment. Divine Love is present today, as always, and expands my awareness and soul presence. I allow my true nature of Divine Essence to be fully expressed.*
>
> *I release any judgments, fears, or animosity to those who are here to awaken me. When I meet others who act in ways that I don't like, I affirm we are all from the same Source. I ask for guidance and support to re-connect with them as a thread of the Holy Oneness.*

Mastery in the Aquarian Era

> *Those who don't feel this Love pulling them, those who don't drink dawn like a cloud of spring water or take in sunset like supper, those who don't want to change, let them sleep.*
>
> Rumi

If you've felt inspired so far from this book on this earth plane—remember or re-commit to your journey as a soul being. You are invited now to step fully into your personal power and personal mastery. You develop personal mastery by expanding yourself emotionally, mentally, physically, and spiritually. Mastery in the Aquarian era involves the ability to understand your material, physical experiences and respond to them <u>energetically</u>. Mastery involves remembering that the energy that flows through you is from Source. Personal mastery in the Aquarian era entails living as a pure expression of Oneness with Source.

As we are learning from cutting edge research within Quantum physics, neurophysiology and other areas of science, the old paradigms for understanding the world are challenged, and need to be revised if not replaced. Studies in mind-body medicine have found that the physical body responds remarkably well to positive affirmations, visualizations, and healing energy. Studies of monks and others highly practiced in meditation have found that their thoughts can affect distant computers, and the thoughts of others sitting in meditation. No longer are cause and effect happening in a linear fashion in time and space. If you want to learn more about these studies, read Lynne McTaggart's fascinating books, *The Field* and *The Intention Experiment*. No longer is this considered "new age mumbo-jumbo", it is the current path for healing, communicating, and working. It is time to learn, practice and master the skills necessary to connect with Source for healing and wholeness around the globe.

When you understand how to function as a spiritual being in a physical world, you not only work through daily challenges more effectively, but you help shift the energy for others around you. This paradigm shift is happening around the globe. More synergy is created as each of us step more fully into the truth and beauty of who we are as soul beings. Many have been draw to greater mastery of spiritual skills for the Aquarian era.

As you master your energy you become more positively potent. You express your innate Divine Essence regularly with family, at work, with neighbors. Personal mastery involves the conscious awareness of being a Divine Expression. Regardless of how challenging the circumstances are, you know you are an infinite radiant being working with abundant flow. You have your feet firmly planted on the ground and your heart fully open to Oneness.

Transformational Empowerment ™

In my work with people addressing life changes and challenges, I've found several spiritual concepts to be invaluable. Aligning your Spirit with your earth walk requires new learning and reconnecting the separate members of Oneness. We weren't given a manual as we entered earth-school of "Five Easy Steps to Soul Consciousness, Inner Peace and Fulfillment". Thankfully, more people around the globe are tuning into their higher vibrational energy and attending to their awakened soul.

Because many people have found the ideas described below to be quite useful for their soul journey, I pulled together teachings that are effective. I developed a process using these teachings, called Transformational Empowerment_{TM}. I offer this process to integrate Spirit as you move through Earth-school.

You probably already use some of these spiritual teachings regularly. Whether you want to transform your work, your health, your relationships, or any other area of your life where you find shifting sand, this process will help you achieve greater confidence, clarity, and power.

Transformation happens when you experience radical and fundamental changes in your life. Empowerment comes when you truly believe that you can affect changes. Transformational Empowerment (TE) happens when you commit to making a positive life change and then take the steps necessary to make it happen.

I named this process "Transformational Empowerment" because it results in deep transformative change. I'm not referring to small changes to feel better momentarily. I'm talking about long lasting and significant shifts, the kinds that are truly transformative in how you think, respond, and live. For most people to live the life they desire, they first need to believe they can make things happen in their life. This requires you to firmly believe that you are a conscious co-creator. Empowerment is the process of believing that change and effort will create a desired outcome. Psychologists refer to this as having a sense of self-efficacy. Without the belief that you can affect change in your life, you won't be motivated to create the life you desire. You have to <u>believe</u> you can achieve your goals and then take the necessary steps towards them.

As you awaken to your soul's calling, you feel the power of those nudges, and know you must address them. It may come from an uncomfortable situation that you need to change or a joyous opportunity that presents itself. If you ignore your soul's urging, the nudges will become louder and stronger. It may feel turbulent at times as you're going through the transformation, but the end result is greater clarity and fulfillment. When was the last time you felt that nudge?

Thich Nhat Hanh reminds us that prayer without action is useless. "The Buddha said—if someone is standing on one shore and wants to go to the other shore, he has to either use a boat or swim across. He cannot just pray, 'Oh other shore, please come over here for me to step across'. To a Buddhist, praying without practicing is not real prayer."

Are you going to stay on the shore where it is familiar, though perhaps no longer comfortable, or will you cross the river? We often stay stuck in the same routines or way of life because it is familiar. Perhaps you are more comfortable staying where you are rather than taking action to step into the unknown. Yet faith involves going to the edge of what you know and taking one more step, knowing that you have the support and guidance that you need. Until and unless you set your heart and mind on doing things differently, you will experience the same challenges in different forms. As an awakened being, you can meet your challenges or make desired changes in your life without having to get to the breaking point.

Often people don't make major changes unless they have to. Inertia is quite powerful. Unfortunately too many people wait for a crisis or until some pain becomes too great. Many people are content to stay on familiar ground, even if they have dreams of other things they want to achieve. What untapped potency! We are all positive powerful forces in the world. You are reading this now because you believe in your ability to shift your positive potential into powerful action. That is personal mastery in the Aquarian era.

Everyone has the ability to transform their reactions and feelings by shifting from lower energy vibrations to higher energy vibrations. This involves releasing old patterns of behavior that don't work and creating newer patterns for wholeness and clarity. Personal mastery for conscious evolution means you know and remember new ways of demonstrating your Divine Essence.

Below is a diagram of the steps towards personal mastery that allow you to create your heart's desire and stay grounded in shifting sand. This process is helpful for anyone who wishes to live with soul consciousness and connection to Oneness. Use this process if you are ready for a new beginning. Share this process with someone ready to expand their power as a spiritual being. For those of you already fully integrating your spiritual path with your worldly path, these teachings are a reminder. Use these for those times when you hit bumps in the road or find the ground below you shifting. You can use these ideas at any time you need to call forth greater energy and turbo-charge your life with Source Energy.

Transformational Empowerment Process

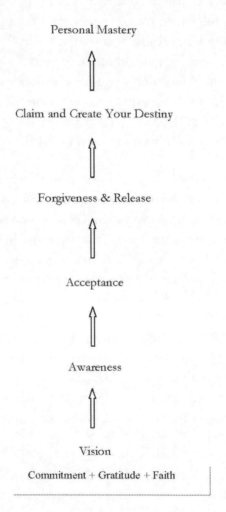

Personal Mastery

Claim and Create Your Destiny

Forgiveness & Release

Acceptance

Awareness

Vision

Commitment + Gratitude + Faith

Though I envision the process as a stepped progression towards personal mastery, in fact you have to continually go back to these teachings as you move to greater radiance. At each step in your soul journey you must stay committed to your process so that you keep energy focused. The more awakened you are to your soul journey, the greater your commitment to living in a way that supports your journey.

In addition to commitment, gratitude and faith are the foundations for creating the life you desire and developing soul-filled Personal Mastery. Being grateful every day for your blessings helps you get through the difficult or uncertain times. Gratitude raises your energy by celebrating life's small and large wonders. Gratitude helps sustain your energy while you change from old to new patterns of living. Gratitude allows you to stay connected to the abundance of love, joy, and peace around you.

> *Gratitude raises your energy by celebrating life's small and large wonders.*

Faith rests in your belief in the Abundant Infinite Radiance. This awareness helps you in those dark wilderness experiences when you feel discouraged or lost. Everyone hits periods of doubt and uncertainty. At times you may think, "What kind of fool have I been to do this!" or "I don't see how I'll get through this one." Seek others who help you remember your connection to Source during these times of doubt. Nay-sayers and your critical inner voice can be quite loud. At times you may feel so slammed to the floor that you have no other choice but to ask your Higher Power for assistance. Stay open to answers and grace-filled experiences. They will be beautiful. Pay attention to seeing them when they are there. They will fill your cup. These three foundation blocks—commitment, gratitude and faith, are essential for each step for personal mastery. They hold you steady and renew your energy as your soul journey unfolds.

I will summarize briefly below the steps from Vision to Personal Mastery. Each foundation block supports the steps. For each element there is a core principle that corresponds to it. In my workshops on the Transformational Empowerment$_{TM}$ process, I provide examples and activities to apply these teachings in your life. Share the ideas presented below with people you know already on the path and ask them how they've used these teachings.

Overview of Transformational Empowerment Process

Foundation Block 1.

<u>Commitment</u>—Commit to fulfilling your soul's yearnings with your whole heart.

Core Principle: ***Feed your Intentions with Attention.***

Foundation Block 2.

<u>Gratitude</u>—Living in gratitude for all that you have helps you to see the gifts in all things/situations. Gratitude connects you to the renewing abundance of God-Sourced Energy.

Core Principle: ***Great Spirit/ Divine Presence is constantly within you and around you. It is the Source of your being.***

Foundation Block 3.

<u>Faith</u>—Rest in the faith that the Sacred Oneness supports your soul journey. Connecting with your Higher Power you draw in your next right highest good.

Core Principle: ***Law of Attraction—Like energy attracts like kind.***

Step 1.

<u>Vision</u>—Develop a clear vision of what you desire to create or shift so you live true to your soul journey Focus on that vision regularly. Have it clear in your mind.

Core Principle: ***Energy flows where attention goes.***

Step 2.

<u>Awareness</u>—Identify those self-limiting beliefs/judgments/ expectations that are blocking you from moving forward. Your thoughts and beliefs drive your actions and affect the energy in your world.

Core Principle: ***You change your world from the inside out. Your thoughts, beliefs and perceptions co-create your reality.***

Step 3.

<u>Acceptance</u>—You are not a victim. You are where you need to be. Now is the time to be a positive potent force in your world.

*Core Principle: **All is in Divine right order for you to experience the radiance and power of your Divine Essence.***

Step 4.

<u>Forgiveness & Release</u>—Let go of your attachments to your self-limiting beliefs, past pain, resentments, and judgments. As you forgive yourself and others, you move forward with more compassion and energy.

*Core Principle: **There is nothing wrong and no one to blame. All people and events in your life are part of your soul journey.***

Step 5.

<u>Claim and Create Your Destiny</u>—Affirm that it is safe, beneficial and holy for you to fully awaken to Who You Are as a soul being.

*Core Principle: **You are here as a Divine Expression to support the conscious evolution of all.***

Step 6.

<u>Personal Mastery</u>—Consciously and intentionally transmute lower energy vibrations to higher energy vibrations with your thoughts, words and deeds. Draw down Source Energy to manifest your heart's desires, fulfill your soul contracts, and celebrate the Oneness.

*Core Principle: **Energy can neither be created nor destroyed, only changed in the form that it takes. You are responsible for how your soul journey unfolds and how you use Source Energy.***

You are reading this book because you are awakened to a deeper calling within yourself and are ready to answer your soul. Thus you are prepared to shift, or already have shifted, your life to be in alignment with that deeper calling. When you remember your soul journey, you experience, feel and know that 'All is in Divine Right Order' even if you can't see the whole picture in the moment. Gratitude keeps your energy high as you endure the hard times and savor the sweet moments. Commitment and faith are the other essential foundation blocks.

Vision and Awareness are the first steps towards Transformational Empowerment. Vision helps you focus your journey. Awareness supports your awakening. As you become aware of previous self-limiting beliefs, you recognize not only when you learned them, but also how they prevent you from achieving what you desire. Your task is to release them and replace them with new beliefs that support your next steps as a soul being. You can't get rid of the negative judgments, perceptions and self-limiting beliefs until you are aware you have them.

Accepting that you are exactly where you need to be in any given moment frees up your energy for consciously co-creating your life as an awakened soul being. Accepting your life <u>as it is</u> helps you move to the **next** highest expression of yourself. Rather than being mired in the "ain't-it-awful game," your energy is directed toward creating your heart's desire and fully expressing your Divine Essence.

Since all is in Divine Right Order, there is no need for judgments of right or wrong, blame or shame. There is no separation; you understand the Oneness paradigm of the Aquarian era. Opportunities have been and continue to be presented for your growth, healing, remembering, joy and love. When you learn to see stressful situations as gifts, you discover the reason for what you are experiencing. This will help you accept rather than struggle with what is occurring in your life.

Feeling and expressing gratitude daily allows you to accept that you have exactly the right circumstances to make the shifts that you want to make in your life. Compassion allows for greater healing, love and conscious evolution. It's a self-feeding process: acceptance feeds compassion, compassion feeds acceptance. Compassion is fuel to boost your energy and feed others.

When you give up thinking about who is "right" or "wrong," you accept others as they are. If you can go one more step to see the situation from a soul perspective, you'll understand the Oneness of all living on the planet. As you understand the soul journey of others more clearly, you find greater compassion and no longer need to feel righteous or victimized. This helps you remove blocks of criticism, judgment, blame, and self-limiting beliefs that otherwise would keep your energy at a lower vibrational frequency.

Through forgiveness and release of old, non-useful patterns of thoughts, words or behaviors, you connect more to the Abundance that flows everywhere. Your soul peels off another layer of useless human conditioning. You walk more lightly, your energy is raised, and you share that lightness with others on the physical plane. Because Like Energy Attracts Like Kind, you draw people and situations towards you that are in alignment with the energy that you radiate. As the saying goes, 'How do you get to Carnegie Hall? Practice, Practice, Practice." Be the Divine Essence that you are and you open your flow of God-Sourced Energy. Channel that Energy to create the life you wish to have, to fulfill your soul contracts, and radiate the Power of Love. Claim your power to co-create heaven on earth. You are not separate but integrated into the fabric of Oneness.

Since Like Energy Attracts Like Kind, resources and situations that align with your soul consciousness start showing up in wonderful unexpected ways. As you become more masterful at directing your thoughts and energy, you get better at creating abundance for yourself and others. The next steps for fulfilling your soul journey are in your hands. Each day is an opportunity to intentionally and joyfully allow the beauty of your Divine Essence to shine forth.

You have seen this happen in your life already. Are you ready to go further living your soul consciousness on a daily basis?

As you get more in touch with your soul journey, finding wholeness and creating joy, you are able to offer your gifts to support others in their journey as well. We are here to support one another in the various ways we each know best. When we better understand our soul contracts with each other, we intentionally offer our gifts for the conscious evolution of all. The transformation of the Aquarian era involves remaining awakened, aware that we are intertwined in a large energetic ecosystem. As we consciously evolve, the whole web of existence shifts accordingly.

The world is waiting for you to powerfully express yourself as an awakened soul being. This is the call and the shift awaiting us in the Aquarian era.

> *The world is waiting for you to powerfully express yourself as an awakened soul being.*

Dancing in Your New Adventure

This transformational work requires openness and vulnerability to honestly address your feelings, needs, and beliefs. Self-reflection requires a high degree of courage and commitment to look at how you are supporting or blocking your own flow of Love. Each day and each moment you have a choice to be fully alive, to awaken to your Divine Expression.

Claiming your soul journey, you ask for assistance from spiritual guides and teachers. You remember to connect with Love in the midst of your daily physical activities. I have used this Sufi chant on several occasions when I've felt scared or unsure: "Only Love is flowing here".

As you embark on making shifts to greater express your radiant essence, you don't waste your time or energy being mad or hurt. By making a commitment to your conscious evolution, you let go of negative judgments of others (or situations or yourself). In this new Aquarian era you begin to see everyone as expressions of Divine Essence and Holy Oneness. You won't need to inflict further pain or to continue your part of the blaming or judging game because you know it does damage to the One of which you are a part. Instead you focus on showing up to your life with more energy, joy, and love.

See how you dance in this joyful new manifestation of Life?

Celebrate that you've gotten this far in your journey. As you practice these ideas for personal mastery, you'll find the steps more comfortable. For those of you already familiar with these ideas, you're probably getting more frequent opportunities to use them or teach them to others. Are you ready to take your soul journey to the next level? Proclaim and step fully into you Who You Are as a 4ᵗʰ Dimensional Being.

Return to your Learning Agreement

You started this book reflecting on your Learning Agreement for coming to Earth-school. Go back to that agreement and see if anything new has emerged for you since reading this book. Re-read your Learning Agreement and revise what you now believe your soul contracts, life purpose, and critical life lessons are. Take some time to see how you can focus your positive potential on your Learning Agreement in the weeks ahead.

You can apply the Transformational Empowerment process to your soul's Learning Agreement. Spend some time reviewing the process and see how it maps onto your Learning Agreement. If there are new opportunities awaiting you, new adventures, new goals on your horizon, use the Transformational Empowerment process to manifest your heart and soul's desires.

For you who are beginners to spiritual manifesting and change, think of a situation or area of your life that needs refining, or a situation that is already shifting for you. It could involve work, relationships, health or other domain of your life. Address the questions at the end of this chapter as it pertains to that issue or situation. Test out these ideas for yourself. See how they work in your life. This is the new Aquarian era way of relating, manifesting, working, healing and being. Personal mastery occurs by working with the Spirit realm for guidance and resources. No longer bound by old notions of spirit and matter, you are free to create in ways never imagined before. Tap into the Energy and enjoy the ride. You'll be amazed at what you experience.

Stepping fully into this new way of living and being, you'll encounter others who are similarly aligned and then greater synergy will be created. It's been such a joy for me to share this work and hear of others doing similar work to bring about transformations on the planet at this time.

Thank you for offering your Light and higher vibrational energy for the healing, comfort, joy, and support of others on this path. This is the Aquarian era. No longer is the paradigm one of scarcity, hoarding, lack or separateness. Rather the new era is about sharing freely, paying it forward, seeing the inter-connected One-ness. We are here to amplify and accelerate everyone's conscious evolution and soul journey. This is an invitation to dance with the Universe, to create greater beauty, joy and peace. All the power that you need to make changes in your life already lies within you—Activate it. Step forward and proclaim your true self to the world.

> *"It is in the unfoldment of the soul that the purpose of life is fulfilled."*
>
> Hazrat Inayat Khan

End of Chapter Exercises

1. Those people who join you on your soul journey become mirrors showing how you want to be or how you are living currently. What are others mirroring for you now? For each person connected to your life today, ask:

    *   *How is this person's good and bad qualities a mirror of who I am?*

    *   *What are the spiritual qualities we are mirroring for each other?*

    *   *What do we celebrate about each other?*

2. What is your grandest vision for who you want to be? How can you practice living that way now, even if only five minutes a day? What will help you be attentive, creative, courageous, committed to bringing this to fruition?

3. Examine one change you wish to make in your life. What support do you have or need to make this shift happen within you? How will you strengthen your spiritual practice to stay connected to Source, your guides, angels or spiritual teachers on a daily basis?

4. As your hot buttons or fears get triggered, do this releasing exercise for any quality or situation where you want to bring peace to your life.

    Bring to mind those perceptions or beliefs that no longer serve you. Proclaim aloud "I am ready, willing, able, and committed to clear out any past programming of _____ that is holding me back. I release all attachments to thoughts, fears, or beliefs that keep me from experiencing my wholeness and healing. I release any judgments that prevent me from being a pure channel of Love. I do this so that the right highest good can be done for me and all other people in my life, now and in the future. Thank you Sweet Spirit. It is so."

About the Author

Dr. Linda J. Ferguson is a seasoned trainer and facilitator, presenting her work around the country and abroad. She provides spiritual life coaching, workshops, and keynote addresses. Linda has been featured in numerous newspapers, magazines, and radio shows. Her previous publications include *Path for Greatness: Work as Spiritual Service,* a chapter for an edited book, *The Workplace and Spirituality: New Perspectives on Research and Practice*, and several articles in the journal, *Interbeing: A Journal of Personal and Professional Mastery*. Linda earned her M.A. in Social Psychology and Ph.D. in Management from Indiana University.

Linda works with spiritually awakened people ready to deepen their spiritual practice and expand their soul journey. She likes to share her gifts for the conscious transformations on the planet. Linda writes a weekly blog on Spirituality and Work available on her website and at *www. managementhelp.org/blogs/spirituality/* Her website **www.lindajferguson. com** has useful resources to assist your spiritual journey.

Linda currently lives in Virginia where she practices and enjoys Sufi Dances of Universal Peace, Shamanic drumming, sacred chanting, Integral yoga, Native American sweat lodges, and Earth-based ceremony. Her spiritual journey has intersected many paths over the last 25 years, gaining insights from various faith traditions. She follows the philosophy that spiritual paths are many, all extending from the same Source.

References

Here are some books that have influenced me over the years and shaped my thinking on the topics covered in this book. This is by no means an exhaustive list of books that have informed my writing, nor is this meant as a bibliography of the books or writing cited in this book. These book references below are offered as a resource for you to explore further the ideas covered in this book.

Brennan, Barbara. 1987. *Hands of Light: A Guide to Healing Through the Human Energy Field*. NY: Bantam Books.

Calhoun, Peter. 2007. *Soul on Fire: A Transformational Journey from Priest to Shaman*. CA: Hay House.

Hanh, Thich Nhat. 1992. *Peace is Every Step: The Path of Mindfulness in Everyday Life*. NY: Bantam Books.

Hick, Esther, and Hicks, Jerry. 2004. *Ask and It is Given: Learning to Manifest Your Desires*. CA: Hay House.

Hubbard, Barbara Marx. 1998. *Conscious Evolution: Awakening Our Social Potential*. CA: New World Library.

Katie, Byron, and Mitchell, Stephen. 2002. *Loving What Is: Four Questions That Can Change Your Life*. NY: Three Rivers Press.

Kornfield, Jack. 2001. *After the Ecstasy the Laundry: How the Heart Grows Wise on the Spiritual Path*. NY: Bantam Books.

McTaggart, Lynne. 2008. *The Field: The Quest for the Secret Force of the Universe*. NY: HarperCollins.

Moore, Thomas. 1992. *Care of the Soul: A Guide for Cultivating Depth and Sacredness in Everyday Life*. NY: HarperCollins.

Myss, Caroline. 2007. *Entering the Castle: Finding the Inner Path to God and Your Soul's Purpose*. NY: Free Press.

Redfield, James. 1993. *Celestine Prophecy*. NY: Warner Books.

Rosenberg, Marshall. 2003. *Nonviolent Communication: A Language of Life*. CA: PuddleDancer Press.

Tenzin Gyatso, The Fourteenth Dalai Lama. 2003. *Compassionate Living*. Boston: Wisdom Publications.

Contacting Dr. Linda J. Ferguson

To schedule a workshop, retreat, presentation,
or coaching with Dr. Linda J. Ferguson

Visit: www.lindajferguson.com

Email: info@lindajferguson.com

Follow Linda on Twitter: @ljfnewprdgm

Friend Linda on Facebook:
http://facebook.com/lindafergconsciouscreator